Couples Therapy and Infidelity Recovery Workbook

The Ultimate Guide to Rebuild, Restore, and Strengthen Your Relationship

Table of Contents

Part 1: Couples Therapy Workbook

Building Trust, Intimacy, and Communication for Thriving Relationships

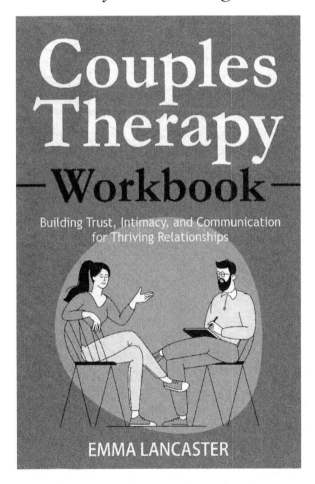

Introduction

Although human beings are one of many kinds of social creatures on this planet, there are important ways in which our interactions differ from those who also inhabit the animal kingdom. People are complicated, and they possess an unprecedented level of self-awareness. As a result, their relationships with others are infinitely more complex and powerful than any other interaction in nature. The depths of communication that human beings are capable of are apparent even in mundane, everyday relationships in daily life. Relationships become much deeper in friendship, but family and romance are where the power of human connection truly comes into its own.

As important and indispensable as romantic relationships are in any fulfilling life, they are not without difficulties. People in meaningful relationships bring all they have to the table, including their complexities. Long-term, intimate relationships are where all of these personal complications eventually come to the forefront, whether you like it or not. For these reasons, even the most worthwhile and fulfilling relationships can become difficult to maintain. Since every individual is unique, relationship difficulties can arise due to an endless array of reasons.

Even though every couple is its own story, luckily, there are many universally effective ways of strengthening and maintaining a relationship. If you're in a relationship that has entered a turbulent phase, know this is common. Most relationships will encounter problems at some point. Still, these issues can and should be resolved because preserving a valuable relationship is a worthwhile struggle. Whatever the crisis, the chances are good that you and your significant other can work through it and come out of these trials with an even stronger bond.

This book will help you and your partner navigate any tumultuous period regardless of your personal situation, character, the duration of your relationship, or any other specifics particular to your couple. Whether you've picked up this book to resolve ongoing problems or are just looking for information on how to improve and strengthen your relationship in general, you will find plenty of guidance and practical advice throughout the following sections. Of all the seemingly irrational aspects of the human experience, love is one that undoubtedly makes life worth living. Yet despite the frequent incomprehensibility of love, you'll find that many things you can do to cherish, nurture, and strengthen love are very practical and rational.

Section 1: It Starts with Trust

It's easy enough to say that love and passion drive romantic relationships. There's no doubt that these ingredients provide the initial spark that brings a couple together. Love and passion are also necessary to keep a long-term relationship going strong over the years. If these are the foundations of a romantic relationship, trust is the key building block that allows couples to continue raising their cathedral of love.

Building a healthy foundation starts with trust.
https://www.pexels.com/photo/man-and-woman-holding-hands-127420/

Love and trust, however, are quite different. Falling in love is a spontaneous force of nature; it flows out from deep within and is often inexplicable. It just happens and feels good, and people rarely have a reason to question such deep and sincere feelings. Trust, on the other hand, takes work. In the first section of this workbook, you will learn the nuances of what trust really is, why it's important, how it can be broken, and the steps you and your significant other can take to rebuild and foster trust.

What Trust Is and Why It Matters

While falling in love can happen with what seems like lightning speed, trust is built up gradually. Some people are naturally more trusting than others and can open up more easily, but building up trust always takes at least some time, even years, in some cases. Trust can grow naturally over that extended period, but building it can also be a conscious effort. Different people might have a million different ways of handling the issue of trust, but one universal truth is that meaningful relationships of all shapes and sizes require trust as an absolute necessity.

It's also true that focusing on trust is just as vital in trustful and functional couples as it is in those who struggle with it. Every relationship style will require both partners to show and justify some level of trust if it's going to work out. Couples that function well together, with partners who are open and sincere with each other, will always have to maintain that trust at a healthy level. Couples who have trust issues, whether they're a couple in therapy or are just having a minor turbulent phase, will have to do a lot of focused work to mend that specific problem.

Since relationships are all about emotional and physical intimacy, they require partners to open up to each other. Without opening up, it's impossible to allow someone to get to know you at a level that's needed for a fulfilling, long-term companionship. To open up to another person entails vulnerability. It requires you to break down your walls, forego your defensive posture, and truly let another person into your world. Most people have at least some natural aversions to such an idea because opening up in this way implies the risk of getting hurt somehow.

Trust occurs when you are able to do this with confidence and a firm belief that no harm will befall you. The essence of trust is feeling safe and comfortable when opening yourself up to your partner or spouse. In that regard, trust can be viewed as a key that unlocks the doors to some of the more sensitive parts of your life. These are the parts on which your partner will have to tread lightly if your relationship's bond is to develop to its full potential. While the aversion to vulnerability is common, most people can get past it spontaneously and without too much effort through the natural process of getting comfortable with someone. This is why folks with trust issues struggle in relationships; this problem can still be conquered.

The existence or lack of trust in a relationship is always strongly felt in any romantic endeavor, as there are numerous ways in which the level of trust manifests itself and shapes the relationship. In relationships built on trust, partners are more comfortable opening up and, as a result, give more to the relationship. When you trust someone, you'll have a much easier time forgiving them for simple shortcomings and mistakes. This allows you to work through problems healthily instead of always doubting your partner and expecting the worst of them.

Conflict is also much easier to deal with when people trust each other. Conflict resolution is all about communication, and this might sometimes require some uncomfortable conversations and the revealing of sensitive feelings and thoughts, which is impossible to do without trust. Navigating many common relationship problems necessitates giving one's partner the benefit of the doubt because human beings will make plenty of minor mistakes in their lives.

Shared interests, physical intimacy, and passion are some of the other things that bring couples together, but trust elevates their closeness and strengthens their bond on a whole new level. Couples built on trust are much closer and tend to know each other better. These feelings of safety and comfort with one's partner will infuse a romantic relationship with a profound friendship that works in unison with romance to create a lasting companionship.

Trusting couples are more self-sufficient because each partner will feel that there is hardly anything they can't discuss with their significant other. They rarely have to go outside of their relationship to seek support or advice. No topics will be off limits for them, which makes it possible to solve virtually any problem. Trust also makes it possible to be confident in all your decisions and plans with your partner. Words need to align with actions in relationships because this builds trust and provides stability, consistency, transparency, and respect.

If your relationship lacks trust, you and your significant other will feel its absence on many fronts. One common manifestation of mistrust is the erosion of personal boundaries. Relationships are about sharing a life with someone else, but healthy relationships always leave some personal space for each individual. Suppose you find it difficult to tolerate any boundaries your partner might like to establish. In that case, you're likely struggling to *trust them*. On the flip side, if your partner is overly invasive and overbearing, it's a clear sign that they have their own trust issues. There are couples where both of these scenarios are true, and an environment like this will almost always create a dysfunctional, toxic relationship.

Accusations, paranoia, and frequent arguments that arise as a result are also strong indicators that your relationship has a trust problem. As previously stated, mistrust makes it very difficult to open up, so there will be a lack of intimacy as a consequence. This can even translate into a lack of physical intimacy and impact the sexual aspect of your relationship. Relationships that lack trust are thus severely unfulfilling on both the emotional and physical fronts. Insecurity, feelings of betrayal, and fears of abandonment will also abound when trust is lacking.

The absence of trust can escalate small issues into misunderstandings and tension in the relationship.
https://www.pexels.com/photo/worried-couple-with-notebook-looking-at-each-other-4246239/

In summary, a relationship built on trust is one where partners or spouses can tell each other anything, ask difficult questions, enjoy occasional personal time without being questioned, and have a rich and fulfilling life of intimacy. This healthy state of affairs results in feelings of security, comfort, peace, and immense emotional fulfillment. It's also the kind of relationship where mistakes can be forgiven and misgivings understood. There is no fear, anxiety, loneliness, insecurity, or unconstructive arguing. Unfortunately, even a perfect relationship can enter a crisis period where trust diminishes. Trust should never be taken for granted and should instead be nurtured and kept from harm at all times.

The Many Enemies of Trust

Strong relationships between trusting and committed partners can weather any storm, and the trust in these relationships is naturally more resistant to challenges. However, it's also true that trust is beset on all sides by a million different curveballs that life can throw at people. These problems can often occur due to a person's previous life experiences that might have nothing to do with their current relationship. On the other hand, there are relationships where things that have damaged trust, such as past breaches of trust, need to be addressed.

Regarding past experiences, some people have just had bad luck with previous partners and, therefore, become insecure. For others, the issues begin in their childhood, which is a time when people are first acquainted with the basics of trust and are supposed to develop healthy attitudes toward it. Everyone begins their life with a natural need to rely on their parents, and the trust that a child feels toward their caregivers and is given in return plays a role in later development.

Excessive, overbearing control by untrusting parents or betrayals of a child's trust by the parents can be equally detrimental. This often leaves lifelong consequences and can cause people to always default to severe mistrust when they grow up. They struggle in relationships because they've never been taught in their formative years that trusting a loved one is a risk worth taking, with the reward being an emotionally fulfilling life. Witnessing mistrust between parents can also make a child grow up with trust issues, even if the child wasn't personally betrayed or treated with mistrust. While trust issues that stem from this source are particularly deeply etched into the mind, they can be resolved with enough dedicated work.

Unfortunately, people with a perfectly healthy upbringing and who are willing to open themselves up can also end up in relationships where trust declines. Even if both partners are like this, other things can happen during a relationship or before that relationship that will lead to mistrust. Betrayal in the current or previous relationship is one of the more common and obvious causes of trust issues. This usually happens through infidelity and can cause massive damage to years of built-up trust. It's not a deep-seated form of mistrust, however, as it's merely an incident that leads to fallout. So, trust can be rebuilt even after such an episode if there is enough will and effort.

Disagreements like clashing personal values or expectations can also damage trust, which happens when a couple has diverging outlooks on life, relationships, and other matters. Communication through meaningful, open conversations can help unite two people regardless of their differences, but it requires an open, non-judgmental environment.

Life experiences that don't relate to trust can also lead to trust issues in relationships. For example, people who have experienced a lot of social rejection can develop significant problems with opening up to others or trusting them. Frequent rejection leaves a lot of bad emotional residue, making people feel unworthy. People with this experience might find it difficult to believe that their partner's intentions are sincere, putting the very nature of the relationship into question. This problem can be exacerbated if a person feels they aren't getting enough validation or is neglected in the relationship.

These and many other problems can also manifest as jealousy, one of the most common obstacles in the way of trust. Jealousy is obvious, easy to identify, and unbearable, but it almost always has an underlying cause. For better or worse, many of these problems result from misunderstandings and communication barriers. This seemingly minor obstacle can cause so much pain, but fortunately, addressing how you communicate with your partner can fix many problems.

Healing, Building, and Nurturing Trust

Establishing trust is a two-way street. Sometimes, the problem is getting yourself to trust your partner, but in other instances, it's about getting your partner to trust you. Problematic relationships come in many forms, and trust isn't always the issue, but it does have to be maintained. Strengthening trust in a smooth, fulfilling relationship can also never hurt. Whatever your situation, the following steps can help smooth things out for you and your significant other in the trust department while strengthening your bond.

Identifying the Problem

Suppose you and your partner know intimately about each other and your lives before meeting. In that case, chances are good that you've already picked up on a few possible causes of mistrust between you while reading this section. Identifying the root of the problem is the first essential step toward addressing it. If you have a solid idea of the problem and are ready to take other steps, but if you just have a vague feeling of an overall lack of trust, you need to ask questions.

Continuous conversation is the key to healthy communication.

Conversation is vital, and different couples will have to ask different questions. If the trust issues stem from previous relationship experiences, then exploring those is a good idea. Be understanding and non-judgmental when doing this because digging around the past can bring all sorts of mistakes and grief to the surface.

Trust-Building Dialogue and the Power of Forgiveness

Engaging in all sorts of trust-building dialogue is how you identify the problem. Still, it's also how you devise a plan of action for you and your partner. One common starter is to discuss with your partner what trust means to both of you. While the definition of trust is universal, people can have significantly different perceptions. Talking about this will help clarify what each of you expects from the other. If you feel like the person who goes first might influence the other, it might be a good idea to write this down and then show it to each other at the same time.

If trust has been breached in the past, this also has to be discussed. It's one of the more difficult endeavors. Still, if you can have a non-judgmental, open-hearted conversation about these incidents, you and your partner will feel better and more confident in your relationship afterward. Reflective questions are also a great asset in conversations about trust. They will help you reflect on your thinking process and how you process certain things. How long have you been together? What was it that brought you together? What is the one thing you struggle with in your partner or yourself? What was it that hurt you the most? Engaging in guided discussions is often used in therapy, formulating a long list of pertinent questions to provoke deep reflection in the couple.

Forgiveness can be a difficult pill to swallow, but it's also severely underrated. If mistakes in your relationship require forgiveness to move forward, you should find it in your heart to make that step. As difficult as it can be, forgiveness is the key to fixing some relationships, and the question is whether you care enough to do it. If you reflect on this question, you will find that reading this book is a testament to the fact that you feel, deep inside, that your relationship is worth saving. If forgiveness is the only way to do that, you should try giving a second chance. The same applies to apologizing.

Commitment Letters

Dialogue is what will help you ascertain what the problems are and what should be done about them. After that, it's up to you and your partner to put those solutions into practice and reinforce your decisions. These solutions can sometimes require radical changes and significant commitments between partners.

To solidify your decisions and make it easier to get started, get your determinations out on paper, such as by writing commitment letters to each other. You and your partner can write down clearly and concisely what you will commit to in order to build trust. It would be a simple and straightforward proclamation that you will stick to.

You can give this a try below:

_____
_____
_____
_____
_____
_____
_____
_____

Trust Scenario Exercises and Regular Trust Check-ins

Great discoveries can be made if you and your partner develop a few fictional, trust-related scenarios to explore how you would think and act if they were to happen. For instance, if your partner has trust issues, you can present them with a hypothetical scenario where you are away on a business trip. Try to get your partner to open up and speak sincerely about what they would be feeling and thinking in that case. This will help you both to articulate the feelings and expectations related to trust in your relationship. Countless hypothetical scenarios can be invented for each specific couple, so it's a good idea to reflect on past arguments and situations where problems have occurred. This will help you develop the most relevant scenarios to explore and discuss.

After enough reflection and deliberation, you and your partner should have an idea of what you expect from each other, what the problem areas are, what trust means to each of you, and what kinds of changes in behavior and thinking you need to make to rebuild trust. It might be helpful to allocate a certain time each week to discuss your trust-related concerns while simultaneously commending your partner for what they did right that week. This would be a sort of debrief where you'd review the week and positively reinforce your trust-building plan. If you and your significant other have a detailed plan with many practical steps, it could be useful to create a weekly checklist of actions and then review each other's scores during the check-in.

Come up with trust-related scenarios and discuss them in depth.
https://www.pexels.com/photo/elderly-people-having-a-conversation-7117581/

Much of your efforts around trust will come down to healthy and meaningful communication. You will learn more about improving communication with your partner or spouse later in this book. Still, it suffices to say that relationships cannot be fixed if you don't talk openly and sincerely. Communication and trust are perhaps the central relationship aspects that permeate most efforts to improve other areas of your love life. Trust and communication will likely play a role in whatever you need to do to improve your love life, as you'll thoroughly learn throughout the rest of this book.

Section 2: How to Navigate Conflict

It's virtually impossible to be in an intimate relationship with someone without encountering at least some conflict. People have different outlooks, values, hopes, expectations, standards, and emotions. The clash of these factors among different people often happens even in mundane, daily relationships, let alone between people who spend years or an entire lifetime sharing their lives.

Conflict is bound to happen, and you must learn how to navigate it.
https://www.pexels.com/photo/couple-quarreling-in-kitchen-8560740/

As such, the difference between solid and dysfunctional relationships isn't that the former has no conflicts. The difference is in the destructiveness and frequency of those conflicts. If you accept that conflict is an inevitable part of the human experience, then the discussion focuses on navigating those conflicts with minimal damage. Navigating conflicts and reducing their negative impact on your relationship is a skill, and this chapter will aim to teach you that skill.

The Nature and Causes of Conflicts in Relationships

Once you understand that conflict is inevitable in long-term relationships and decide to learn how to handle it properly, the first thing to take to heart is that conflict shouldn't necessarily be feared. When you know how to process a conflict constructively, it becomes a fixable problem and might even present certain opportunities. Working around these issues inevitably improves communication and understanding. Getting through a conflict can strengthen a relationship, whether a marriage or anything else. Relationships fall apart not because of conflicts but because of what people do during those conflicts.

The trigger and true cause behind a conflict are two very different things. A trigger sets off a heated argument at a given moment. Still, the real reason conflicts happen is usually something underlying. People's personality types, communication styles, and personal stories will all play a role here, especially any personal issues associated with these factors. Extroversion and introversion, for instance, can produce their own conflicts. Introverted people might find it more difficult to open up, leading to frustration in their partner. On the other hand, extroverted people might not be as reflective as their partner would like them to be.

There are several personality type analysis systems out there that might offer further insights in this regard. For instance, the Myers-Briggs Type Indicator (MBTI) is a popular way of analyzing how 16 different personality types think and engage with the world around them. It's a straightforward questionnaire you can find online and fill out with your partner. MBTI isn't the most scientific analytical system out there, but there is no question that it has helped millions of people learn more about themselves. At the very least, it can provide a useful basis for you to start asking the right questions and reflect. The results could point you toward understanding more about why your personalities sometimes clash and where there might be room for compromise.

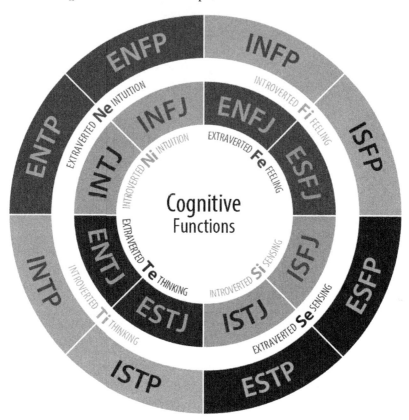

The Myers-Briggs Type Indicator (MBTI) is a popular way of analyzing how 16 different
personality types think and engage with the world around them.
Jake Beech, CC0, via Wikimedia Commons
https://upload.wikimedia.org/wikipedia/commons/e/e6/CognitiveFunctions.png

Apart from personality types and communication styles, a range of
personal and general life issues can arise and lead to conflict. Some
common causes of conflict are those that don't necessarily originate in
either of the partners. However, how people handle these problems can
lead to conflict situations. Responsibilities around the home, money
troubles, substance abuse, and problematic relatives can all infringe upon
a relationship and cause tensions through no fault of the couple.

How the relationship is set up can also cause problems, such as if one
partner feels too powerless and controlled or feels they're sacrificing and
investing too much with no reciprocation from their partner or spouse.
Some relationships can function on an uneven plain, but all people will

require some kind of balance to feel comfortable. Poor communication, which is a problem in and of itself, can make these issues much worse. Partners can sometimes be unaware that they are too controlling or don't contribute enough because their significant other doesn't communicate their needs and expectations correctly.

Expectations can frequently become the epicenter of conflict in relationships. Most of the time, this happens either because one partner is making no effort to meet the other's expectations or because one of the partners has unrealistic expectations. The latter scenario will produce the same feelings in the unsatisfied partner as the former. This is because some find it difficult to differentiate between their unreasonable expectations and their partner putting in the effort. As always, this problem is solved through communication. One side needs to commit to doing their best while the other has to potentially adjust their expectations and ensure they're not smothering their partner with unrealistic standards.

Selfishness is another common pitfall in relationships. It can manifest in many ways, such as jealousy or neglect, but it's often an issue rooted in someone's background. Selfishness can lead a person to neglect their relationship and focus too much on things like work, but it can also cause one partner to require too much attention, leading to a lot of friction and dissatisfaction.

Conflicts can also crop up regularly due to quiet, built-up resentments. The irony is that such a sorry state of affairs can result from misguided attempts to avoid conflict at all costs. When your partner says or does something that offends or disappoints you, the best thing to do is talk about it honestly and openly. The urge to keep quiet to avoid an argument is completely understandable but leads to unresolved negative emotional residue. Not pointing these things out ensures that the problematic behaviors continue. Over time, the seed of resentment will develop, leading to conflicts much worse than a constructive discussion about your expectations and simple things that bother you in your relationship.

These are only a few examples of things that can go wrong, but relationship conflict has as many variables as human relationships. You can also apply a regular analytical approach to understanding the conflicts with your partner. For instance, you can keep a written record of your conflicts. This will make it easier to identify any patterns you might have missed or common triggers that lead to conflict with your significant other. This information is very helpful when trying to devise conflict resolution strategies.

You can try it by writing down the last conflict you remember in the space below. Try to pinpoint when and why it began, how it progressed, and how it ended. Conflicts often have a deep-seated, underlying cause, but it's a good starting point to at least identify the trigger and then take it from there. Analyzing the conflict with your partner can also lead to valuable, unexpected insight and feedback.

This is a good place to start, but if your relationship experiences frequent conflicts, you could perhaps dedicate a notebook or some other planner where you will write down the specifics of every conflict and maintain a permanent collection of such records. It can be useful to go back in time and compare notes to catch wind of any changes for better or worse. Either way, you'll want to keep previous incidents on record if you are to conduct a proper post-conflict analysis, especially when looking for patterns. It's important to stress that such notes should not be used as a 'gotcha' moment with your partner – but rather as a referencing method to avoid the same issues that plague your relationship.

In general, conflict in relationships mostly boils down to issues with communication. While it's inevitable and can happen for an endless range of reasons, the breakdown in communication makes conflict worse and ensures that its negative effects persist over time. As you can see in the above examples of the typical causes of conflict, a lack of communication is a common pattern of the problem, while healthy communication is the cure.

Self-Control and Understanding

The way you listen and communicate your concerns are two of the most important aspects of conflict resolution. When things get heated, try to stay level-headed while retaining respect for your partner and their point of view. To be more precise, conflict situations will require techniques for de-escalation to calm things down and minimize damage, as well as empathy to understand where your partner is coming from and what the conflict is about.

Communication Style Assessment

If you have frequent arguments with your partner, and especially if you've identified patterns during your post-conflict analysis, this can go a long way toward helping you get a better understanding of how you and your partner communicate. To manage conflict situations better, you'll want to thoroughly assess your and your partner's communication styles. Renowned American psychologist, professor, and therapist John Gottman provided valuable insights on this topic.

Gottman has devised the *Four Horsemen of the Apocalypse*. These four communication styles most frequently get in the way of constructive discussion and conflict resolution. Gottman's Four Horsemen include the following:

1. **Criticism** – Being overly critical toward one's partner in a very negative sense. Judgmental attitudes and character attacks.

2. **Contempt** – Treating one's partner with contempt, verbally or through non-verbal cues, demeaning them, and asserting superiority.

3. **Defensiveness** – Often manifested as a lack of willingness to assume responsibility for mistakes and instead pinning the blame on one's partner.

4. **Stonewalling** – Refusing to engage, giving the silent treatment, and generally shutting one's partner out.

In Gottman's research, a pattern of these communication styles effectively predicted divorces and breakups, assuming that the problems remain unaddressed. This is why engaging in the aforementioned post-conflict analysis is necessary, even if you must write it down. If you find that you or your partner engages in the above behaviors, you must address this together. Spotting these behaviors in someone else is easier than in yourself. Both of you need to reflect and ask yourselves whether you're contributing to conflict.

Below is a checklist of a few other ways the Four Horsemen can manifest during conflict. Next time you analyze a conflict, see how many of these you've exhibited, and ask your partner to do the same.

- Starting many sentences with "You."
- Accusations that your partner always or never does a particular thing.
- Attacks on the partner's character by pointing out flaws to insult, not to discuss the issue.
- Digging around the closet for past skeletons and grievances.
- Mocking.
- Sarcasm.
- Condescension.
- Assumptions, especially negative ones, about your partner's thoughts, intentions, feelings, or something similar.
- Aggressive, dismissive, or passively aggressive non-verbal cues like eye-rolling, forceful sighing, and scoffing.
- Any kind of insult, including name-calling.
- Saying things just to cause pain, especially things you don't mean. This usually causes regret later.
- Defaulting to excuses instead of evaluating and accepting personal responsibility.
- Never admitting any wrongs.
- Elaborate justifications of mistakes.
- Stressing the things you hate about your partner or even listing them.
- Cutting off the conversation
- Looking for an escape during arguments.
- Sweeping problems under the rug.
- Difficulty with articulating emotions or thoughts and expressing them.

Emotion Identification, Active Listening, and De-Escalation

When you and your partner are done analyzing a conflict and going through the above checklist, it's time for reflection and exploration. With a non-judgmental approach that puts criticisms aside, this can be an excellent activity for emotion identification. The first step is to consult with your partner by showing them which bits you've checked on the list and asking them if they agree that you did these things and vice versa.

This is a time for empathy, and it will help you identify many of the emotions at play during the conflict. When your partner says you've done a certain thing they dislike, don't immediately default to disagreeing with their assessment, even if you strongly feel that they're wrong. Instead, you want to engage in active listening, which means showing a genuine interest in their point of view, being empathetic, and respecting their thoughts.

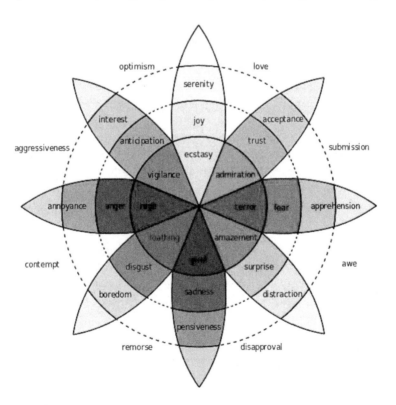

This emotion chart will help you identify many emotions that you may not be able to figure out at times.

Encourage them to divulge more of their perspective by using verbal and non-verbal cues to be as responsive as possible while you listen. If they lay out their case constructively and you still disagree with their assessment, perhaps you'll be able to identify some of the negative behaviors in their feedback. Active listening is about encouraging your partner to open up more and more. When they're done with a statement, you should ask them open-ended questions or try to summarize what they said to see if you understood them. This is how you get to the root of the emotional factors behind your issues. These conversations could also be a great addition to your conflict diary, next to your summaries and analyses of previous conflicts.

While the above exercises mostly involve understanding your conflicts and resolving them for the long term, keeping these things in mind should also assist with de-escalation in the heat of the moment. So, acquaint your partner with what you've learned here as soon as possible if you're having frequent conflicts. You can try to keep the communication style assessment checklist in mind and do the opposite of those behaviors next time you get into an argument.

A simple change in communication, such as opting to start your statements with "I" instead of an accusatory "You," can be surprisingly effective at calming things down. For instance, "You always make me feel worthless" has a much more hurtful connotation than "I feel like I deserve more respect from you." This is much more likely to elicit a positive and reflective response that leads to deep thoughts and introspection in your partner, especially if you are caught in a vicious cycle of conflict.

If the situation allows, conflicts can also be de-escalated through time-outs. If things get too heated, try going to another room for a few minutes to collect your thoughts and calm down. After that, you can come back and pick up where you left off, but now with a cooler head and perhaps a few good ideas on how to proceed. If you can do this, you and your partner already possess a substantial level of self-control you can build upon.

The Importance of Compromise

When things are back under control, and you start getting a handle on the problem, it's time for the finer touches. This means efforts to find common ground and negotiate, which is how conflicts are resolved in the long term. This is the way for you and your significant other to find real, sustainable solutions and reinforce the foundations of your relationship. It's how you find things to agree on and make steps toward minimizing conflict in the future.

Negotiations and Common Ground

To find common ground and identify which compromises can or must be made, you simply have to talk, perhaps more than ever. Finding common ground starts as a game of elimination. You and your partner should identify negotiable and non-negotiable things for you. That which is non-negotiable can then be eliminated and taken off the table. Personal values are a common example.

It's good to reflect together on some of the things you have in common that bring you closer, especially positive things. Starting with the fact that you both care about the relationship and each other is a valuable reminder that love exists between you. When you start on that path and go where it takes you, it quickly becomes clear that you have a lot of common ground.

From that point on, it's all about focusing on the problem you've identified through previous exercises and seeing what both of you can contribute to its resolution. Compromise means that both sides will give something to the cause in the interest of a higher goal. You both have to know what you need and want and listen attentively to each other.

In a joint effort, you and your partner should identify as many things you agree on as possible. You both want fewer arguments, which is a good foundation to build on. What is it that needs to change for you to get there? If you've successfully identified and thoroughly discussed the causes of your arguments, potential solutions should emerge. This is where negotiation comes into play because solutions entail changes and alternatives likely to impact you or your partner in some way.

Finding compromise in any relationship also has much to do with balancing personal and relationship needs. Relationship needs are required to keep your relationship going strong, and they are the needs that will often require some adjustments or sacrifices on the personal front. Compromise is how those sacrifices can be minimized. For example, a conflict might arise over a hobby that a spouse enjoys but spends a lot of personal time on. The other spouse will voice this concern in a way that doesn't just demand the cessation of said hobby but suggests adjustments. A compromise in this situation would be to take up that or some other hobby together or to adjust the schedule.

All of this should be enough to get a foot in the door and start gradually addressing the root causes of your conflicts while learning ways for your partner and yourself to handle yourselves better when conflict does arise. Don't be discouraged if you still struggle to communicate and practically apply what you've learned in this chapter. Later in the book, you will learn all about communication specifically.

Section 3: Increasing Intimacy

Since romantic relationships are all about sharing your life as completely as possible with another person, your ability to be close to each other without holding back is critical for the relationship's success. Knowing someone intimately and being very close emotionally occurs outside of romantic relationships, too. Familial relationships, or even those between close/lifelong friends, have their own kinds of intimacy.

The road to everlasting intimacy takes work in any relationship.
https://unsplash.com/photos/man-and-woman-facing-6rKkr2fh2-I

However, romance is where intimacy takes on its most evolved form, partly because love makes people more susceptible to being vulnerable. Still, there's also the question of physical intimacy. The intricacies of romantic relationships can lead to unusually complex interpersonal issues. So, these relationships require a special emphasis on intimacy. This is precisely because intimacy leads to openness, emotional comfort, security, and vulnerability.

All of these are prerequisites for truly sincere, healthy, open communication, allowing trust to flourish and resolving conflicts. Since intimacy is such a critical aspect of a fulfilling relationship, this chapter will look at some insights into how you and your partner can deepen and enhance your intimacy.

Intimacy in Romantic Relationships

Intimacy in romantic relationships occurs when you and your partner feel profoundly close to each other and have a deep connection. People with this level of intimacy between them also have an intimate knowledge of each other, which enables understanding and perhaps the highest manifestation of empathy that human beings are capable of. Intimacy is often associated with the sexual aspect of relationships and is sometimes mistakenly used as a synonym, but it's much more than that and comes in many forms. All of these forms are equally important. To properly understand how intimacy plays a part in a relationship, it's best to break it down into a few particularly common forms, specifically in romantic relationships.

Physical Intimacy

Physical intimacy in a relationship relates to a couple's sex life, of course, but it's also about much more than that. Couples who are in a functional, fulfilling relationship have their own physical language of gestures and contacts that reinforce the intimate nature of their relationship regarding their overall closeness, not just sex.

There exists a very natural need that we all have for physical touch, which is why even the most mundane physical contacts that have nothing to do with sexual intercourse will spark up your love hormones like oxytocin. Oxytocin is one of the reasons physical contact fosters a feeling of closeness, and it occurs not just in romantic relationships but also between parents and children and in other close relationships. Oxytocin is colloquially known as the love hormone but can also be seen as the connection hormone. Oxytocin leads to feelings of comfort, fulfillment, and calm between people who love each other. It is why humans enjoy cuddling, holding hands, massages, and other similar contact, in addition to sexual interactions.

Emotional Intimacy

Emotionally intimate couples find it easy to express themselves and open up because these are relationships where vulnerability is rewarding and carries no risk of being hurt. Emotional intimacy makes you feel validated and understood when you open up to reveal your innermost feelings and thoughts.

Many people learn emotional intimacy through a healthy upbringing, but it's never too late to improve it. Couples that lack emotional intimacy usually have a diminished sense of security and safety. Of course, trust plays a major part in this aspect of relationships. If you find that whenever you're in a state of distress, your first thought is to talk about it with your spouse or partner, that's a good sign that you are emotionally intimate with them.

Intellectual Intimacy

Intellectual intimacy makes partners relate to each other through shared interests, hobbies, and similar passions. It's also called mental intimacy because it's all about having an intimate understanding of how your partner thinks. This type of intimacy is common between people who share a bond in all types of relationships, not just romantic ones.

Still, romantic partners will always find that being intellectually intimate makes their bond stronger and more exciting. While being emotionally and physically intimate is crucial in all romantic relationships, some people find intellectual intimacy more important than others. It always helps make a relationship more interesting, so it can't hurt. Still, some will actually build their entire relationship around shared intellectual interests. This is because some individuals are naturally attracted to intelligence, and the idea of sharing everything that has to do with work, hobbies, activities, studies, and other similar pursuits with their partner is what they look for. Those who are attracted to intellectual intimacy in a partner are referred to as *sapiosexuals.*

Spiritual Intimacy

This form of intimacy is also somewhat broad, as it can relate to anything from religion to values, ethics, or overall life philosophy. Spiritual intimacy leads some people to believe they've found a "kindred spirit" or "soul mate" in their partner. Spiritual intimacy occurs in various settings and relationships, but it also does well in romantic relationships. If two romantic partners share similar beliefs, they will likely share quite a few things in their worldview and life outlook.

This kind of connection is valuable because it can help people in a relationship find common ground more easily, agreeing on the ways they want to live their lives and what to pursue. Couples find spiritual intimacy through religion, volunteering, reading, or more modern activities such as yoga. Some couples can function without always aligning their values and beliefs, but disagreements can lead to conflict.

Experiential Intimacy

As its name suggests, experiential intimacy is about a couple's experiences together. This kind of intimacy is quite easy to build up, as it only requires you and your partner to take up new activities together, which can be leisurely, work-related, or anything else. The important thing is to share those experiences.

Engaging in activities together builds upon the foundation of your relationship.
https://unsplash.com/photos/couple-sitting-on-edge-while-looking-at-the-mountains-vWqK0KsNTXQ

Engaging in activities you are both interested in is a great way to spend time, but new experiences can be an opportunity to grow closer to your partner. For instance, it's not uncommon for one partner to enjoy something the other partner knows almost nothing about. Joining your partner or having them join you for these experiences can teach you new things about your partner and life overall.

These are only a few of the ways in which intimacy manifests in relationships. The common theme among all these forms of intimacy is that they lead to a stronger bond and tend to have a pleasant, calming effect on you. When you feel truly comfortable and at peace when engaging in or talking about any of the aforementioned moments of intimacy, you know that you and your partner have a truly special bond.

Problems in the Way of Intimacy

At this point in the book, you can probably begin to see how many relationship problems and solutions to those problems tend to feed into each other. For instance, it's clear that a lack of communication will impact a couple's ability to be intimate the way they need to be. It can also be the other way around, with a gradual loss of intimacy leading to more conflict, distance, and an overall breakdown in communication.

Stress and Sex Life

While intimacy isn't all about sex, a loss of sexual intimacy is indeed one of the more common problems. One of the most frequent causes of problems in sexual and other forms of intimacy is stress. Stress can be related to the relationship itself. Still, it's also unfortunate that stress from other parts of your life can seep into your relationship or marriage and build walls where there were none before. People who are stressed out find it difficult to relax in most settings. Suppose you or your partner are feeling uncomfortable and constantly worrying in general. In that case, it's no surprise that it might also reflect on your relationship.

Stress is especially harmful to a couple's sex life because of its effects on the sex drive. Men are especially vulnerable to stress in this regard. More often than not, stressors in a person's life, such as problems at work or financial troubles, lead to chronic tension every day. The problem occurs when a person starts looking for ways to handle their stress and ends up going for solutions other than sex, such as sleeping or engaging in other activities.

A particularly troublesome complication in such a scenario is if the other partner interprets the lack of interest as an indication something is wrong with them. This can produce insecurity, friction, or even resentment. Spicing things up in the bedroom to increase interest can work sometimes, but it can also backfire. It's best to focus on the true cause behind the stress and tackle it directly instead of just wrestling with the symptoms. Suppose you or your significant other is struggling with something in or outside your relationship. In that case, you must talk about it and help each other shake off that burden. Otherwise, walls might start building up between you.

Obstacles to Overall Intimacy

Speaking of walls, a lack of communication can ruin a relationship's intimacy more thoroughly than miscommunication and conflicts. Despite its potential destructiveness, the conflict will at least raise some passion. In some cases, negative communication can be better than no communication. When partners shut each other out, become unresponsive, and stop sharing their problems, little can be done to increase intimacy before reigniting communication.

If there are frequent arguments, those should be addressed in the ways discussed earlier. If there is no communication at all, something has to be done to get it flowing again, even if it initially leads to tensions. Getting communication going from scratch might sound daunting, but a lot can be done, as you'll learn later in this book.

Busy schedules are another interfering factor that can chip away at your relationship over time. Work and children tend to be the primary factors that make couples too busy to spend quality time with each other. If you've had this experience and suspect it has infringed upon the intimacy between you and your partner or spouse, it's an issue you must address. When work and children work in unison to fill up your schedule, there is no shame in seeking help regarding child care, for example. Paying a babysitter or asking a relative to watch the kids at least once a week so you can enjoy some quality alone time can do wonders.

Get a babysitter to allow you to have quality time together without the kids.
https://www.pexels.com/photo/a-woman-story-telling-with-two-children-in-bed-6974747/

Perhaps the most elusive of all intimacy's enemies are *various personal issues*. These can be difficult to deal with when one of the partners won't share their problems, but even when they do, such issues can be severe and require lots of work. These include things like self-esteem problems, past trauma, a painful upbringing, personal tragedies, and a range of physical or mental health problems. Sometimes, seeking professional help to work through these troubles is necessary and should under no circumstance be regarded as shameful.

Strengthening and Nurturing Intimacy

Once you understand intimacy and its enemies, it'll be easier to determine whether your relationship is lacking in that department. If improving and maintaining a satisfying level of romantic intimacy had to be boiled down to three main components, those would be communication, physical contact, and quality time spent together.

Defining Intimacy as an Exercise

A great place to start your journey toward reigniting the spark is to simply sit down with your partner and discuss intimacy. As a simple exercise, you can make an evening out of it. Over dinner or some other comfortable setting conducive to conversation, you could both take your turn trying to best define what intimacy really means for each of you.

As you've seen above, the basic definition of intimacy is straightforward enough, but there's still a lot about intimacy left to the individual's perception and expectations. The end goal is always to be closer to the person you love. Still, in pursuit of that goal, some people might put an emphasis on sex. In contrast, others might think deep conversations or shared new experiences are more important. Intimacy is a feeling, so you must think back and identify situations where you felt the most open, connected, and comfortable with your partner. Those will be the situations and interactions that probably mean the most to you regarding intimacy.

For instance, you and your partner can think up or write your own lists of all the things you feel would increase intimacy and should be added to your relationship. You can let your imagination run wild because the list can include realistic and unrealistic things. The key goal is to give your partner a better idea of how you perceive intimacy.

Sensual Exploration

As mentioned, the role of physical touch, both sexual and non-sexual, is vital to romance. Try to imagine a stereotypical happy couple and how they interact with each other. There are hundreds of non-verbal cues that couples use, mostly unconsciously, to express their affection. They constantly touch each other, teasing, scratching, caressing, leaning on each other, smooching, and much more. These things are really second nature for people who are in love and have a healthy intimacy level.

Physical touch is a major part of how human beings communicate with each other in all manner of relationships and interactions. It's about much more than sharing information, though. It's long been known that the amount of physical touch a baby gets from the mother affects how the child will develop. The role of non-sexual physical touch in romance has also been studied, and it has been shown that couples who casually touch each other all the time report feeling more satisfied and intimate in their relationships. Studies have confirmed what everyone could always see; however, observing a happy and unhappy couple sitting next to each other can really speak volumes.

While this stuff comes instinctively to most people, couples who have lost the spark can and should relearn it. Activities that will allow you and your significant other to engage in the basic sensual exploration of each other are plentiful. It can be as simple as having a movie night together in bed. You might have to remember to cuddle at first, but soon enough, you'll find that it happens on its own as intimacy grows.

Reinvigorating Intimacy through Activities

Hobbies and other activities will always boost a couple's experiential intimacy. Still, depending on the activity, this can simultaneously improve intimacy on many levels. You really can't go wrong with new hobbies that you and your partner find interesting and engaging. As long as it's a constructive, healthy activity, it can only help.

Remembering that date nights aren't just for newly formed couples is important. Most relationships start with regular dates, so returning to such simple activities can refresh a longtime relationship. It can be a nostalgic experience that brings up good old memories and excitement. A fancy dinner once a week is a good opportunity to unwind and foster communication, and a new outdoor activity could reinvigorate both of you mentally and physically.

A dinner date is a great way to switch things up and connect intimately away from your usual surroundings.

The options are endless, but the important thing is that you both enjoy these activities and feel comfortable with them. Sitting down and coming up with new, exciting ideas for all the things you could do together is an excellent and therapeutic exercise in and of itself. It'll encourage you both to open up about the things you want to do and experience, and it might even remind you of all those things about your partner that made you fall in love in the first place.

Make a Weekly Schedule

Some couples can easily jump into new activities with a degree of spontaneity, but a more structured approach could work better for others. Creating a schedule is particularly helpful for busy couples. As an exercise, you and your partner can sit down to discuss ideas for activities you'll enjoy. Afterward, you can run these against both of your weekly schedules to agree on a time that suits you.

You can use the template below to create a very simple weekly schedule, putting in a time for each day and a brief description of the activity you've got planned. It's normal if you aren't able to set aside time every single day of the week, so don't let that discourage you. Some days can be rounded off with a simple yet special dinner at home at the end of the day, accompanied by meaningful discussions. Remember, if you're working on problems like communication and engaging in exercises found throughout this book, those will also work as intimacy-building activities.

Monday:

Activity:

Tuesday:

Activity:

Wednesday:

Activity:

Thursday:

Activity:

Friday:

Activity:

Saturday:

Activity:

Sunday:

Activity:

Section 4: Master the Art of Communication

As you've seen in the previous sections, communication is a matter that comes up repeatedly regarding overcoming problems in a relationship. In essence, a relationship is a form of communication between two people, but it can attain a level of intimacy seldom seen in other forms of human relationships. In a way, a romantic relationship as a manifestation of communication is a special language; the only people who understand it are the two who share that special bond.

Communication is the answer to any tension that might be building up within the relationship.
https://www.pexels.com/photo/cheerful-multiracial-couple-looking-at-each-other-3776877/

When communication breaks down, and barriers are erected, the couple begins to lose that special understanding, and they eventually forget how to relate to each other the way they did before. No matter how strong the bond is between two people in love, communication must be nurtured and preserved. While you've already learned quite a few things about communication in relationships, this section will take a closer look at what communication should look like, what common issues it might face, and how to foster it with your significant other.

What Healthy Communication Looks Like

Suppose you see communication as the transfer of information and consider your relationship a system that relies on accurate, unfiltered, and comprehensible information. In that case, it's easy to understand the practical value of effective communication. Communication is the essence of any attempt to improve human relationships, and most other efforts will be in vain without it.

You must understand what healthy communication looks like if you are to define what problems you might have and which goal you'll be pursuing. If healthy communication had to be summed up with a single concept, that concept would be comfort. One of the first questions to reflect on is whether there are topics or concerns in your relationship that induce any level of anxiety when you think about discussing them with your partner. If you feel anything might be off limits for some reason or supposedly better left unsaid, you and your partner probably aren't communicating on the best frequency.

Comfort in communication exists when there's no question you're afraid to ask and no topic you are reluctant to bring up. When healthy communication is established, you will feel your partner is the one person you can lean on and expect to engage you with understanding, empathy, and patience. Not every topic is right, and some are not worthy of discussion, but that doesn't matter in a healthy relationship. Everything can be talked about, and all issues can be ironed out well before they develop into something worse.

In healthy communication styles, partners are on an equal footing. They don't speak over each other, interrupt, or demean what the other side is saying. They will take turns and constantly encourage each other with feedback, thus facilitating sharing. Both parties will maintain a degree of self-awareness, being mindful of their actions and how their behavior

---

and mode of expression might affect the other side. As section two of this book describes, active listening is an integral part of this process.

Honesty and kindness are some of the clearest signs two people communicate properly. Being truthful in relationships is about much more than just telling the truth about relatively unimportant things. Never telling lies is very important, of course, but in intimate relationships, silence can be a lie in and of itself. The problems people ignore -and the important things they leave unsaid - can damage or completely destroy a relationship, regardless of how long it has been.

Getting over your anxiety to bring up certain things is one side of the coin. Still, the other is making sure that you don't do anything to cause the same problem in your partner. Sometimes, it can be difficult to determine whether another person is being open about their thoughts and feelings, but it's much easier to see these things in someone you know very well. Body language can be a major indicator of how comfortable someone feels during communication. Stable eye contact, open body postures, relaxed sitting, physical direction, and other similar cues are signs that someone is comfortable in an interaction.

How concerns are raised can also provide insight into the quality of communication between you and your partner. There is a big difference in results between raising concerns in a hostile, judgmental, or insulting manner and opening up the conversation with kindness and empathy. A common way to express concerns healthily is to intertwine the negatives with positive, reinforcing speech that reminds your partner that you appreciate them.

For instance, dysfunctional relationships see instances where people will just tell their partner that they hate a certain thing they do, focusing intensely on the negativity in the situation. On the other hand, a considerate, loving partner will tell their significant other that they love and respect them, outlining some of their virtues and positive qualities that they appreciate. Then, they will add the part that bothers them.

Clarity, active listening, empathy, and patience are the building blocks of healthy communication. People who communicate with ease are kind, succinct, and easy to understand. These couples have no problem getting to the point of the matter, and they are able to do so without emotional damage and friction, even when dealing with the most difficult topics.

Common Pitfalls

Something to focus on is the balance between speaking and listening. Suppose you often give prolonged monologs or rants without meaningful feedback. In that case, your partner isn't participating in the conversation on the level they should be. Conversely, suppose you're always playing the listener and can't get a word in. In that case, you're the one who isn't getting the opportunity to express yourself. Both of these imbalances can occur due to either the speaker's aggressiveness or the listener's excessive passivity.

Another common cause of communication problems is the reality of substance abuse and addiction in general. Typical symptoms associated with addiction include a lot of behaviors that make it difficult to communicate sincerely and openly. People who struggle with these issues are often dishonest and refuse to accept responsibility for their mistakes. They also tend to be extremely defensive, deflective, anxious, aggressive, and outright abusive.

On a positive note, addiction and substance abuse are easy to identify, so it's not difficult to determine what must be done. The trouble is that the problem can be rough in some cases. If you and your partner are dealing with these issues, seek out professional help or the assistance of family members. As always, though, it has to start with communication. If your partner is the one with a problem, the first step is to get through to them and convince them that the problem is real and requires solutions.

Whether you do this alone or with someone else's counsel, one of the more effective strategies is to convince your partner that what they are doing is destroying your relationship. Unfortunately, extreme cases might require you to give them an ultimatum, but this can backfire if it's done with judgment and hostility. Instead, their wake-up call needs to be rooted in the love and understanding for you (as their partner) and demonstrate that you're coming from a place of concern and empathy.

There are also many smaller issues in the way people communicate that make it difficult to get the point across. Assumptions are frequent communication mistakes that can obscure the truth and discourage the other side from engaging further, especially when assumptions are seasoned with hostility, judgment, and other negative reactions. Assuming too much and jumping to conclusions is a force of habit for many people, and the antidote is listening while being patient.

Similarly, generalizations should also be avoided. The problem with generalizing things is that it obscures the finer details of the discussion. Generalizations can be avoided if you always remember to remember their positive traits and give your partner credit where it's due. For instance, if your partner has developed a bit of a gambling habit lately, you shouldn't let this one problem overshadow everything else you love about them. Acknowledging their positive traits will make them feel appreciated and more likely to listen to constructive criticism and advice.

Steps to Improve Communication

Putting aside mental health problems, it's always possible to learn how to communicate properly. This is true even for those who've had deep-seated issues throughout their lives and always struggled to communicate effectively. The overwhelming majority of people don't have what might be considered crippling communication issues, though. In most cases, it's a matter of some adjustment and exercise with the goal of improving their communicative skills. This is something that can be done without too much effort daily, and the following tips and exercises could be of help.

Creating Optimal Conditions

If you find it difficult to communicate with your significant other openly and without inhibitions, there are practical steps to set up optimal conditions for a conversation. When communication is particularly bad, talking about the problem is somewhat of a "Catch-22" situation since the problem itself requires a discussion. So serious discussions will go smoother if you and your partner put some effort into how, when, and where you'll talk.

For instance, timing is everything when you need to have a serious talk, and this is the case for couples at all levels of severity in their communication troubles. It goes without saying that some issues should not be raised in heated moments of tension. What's important is that both you and your partner discuss your issues with cool heads, so it's a good idea to ease into important conversations when you're having a particularly relaxed and comfortable time with each other.

The physical setting can play a huge role as well. Outside of therapy and counseling, this should be a private conversation at home or anywhere else you might find peace and quiet. Going to a calm and relaxing place with emotional significance for your relationship can also be beneficial. Lots of couples have places that they are attached to in some way, usually because it was the place where they met, spent some of their best times, or had some other pleasant memory associated with it.

The main goal should be to create a safe environment where both of you will be comfortable enough to open up and share your innermost feelings, thoughts, concerns, or anything else that can help sort things out. This applies to any topic or issue that needs to be resolved through conversation.

Communication in the Digital Era

It's no secret that the digital era and its many innovations have made it possible to communicate at dizzying speeds. This has had some dramatic effects on human relationships, romantic or otherwise, and that's not even the full impact yet.

Texting, for instance, is a very convenient way to keep in touch, but it can become overbearing in relationships. When you text too much all day, the habit can leave you worried when the slightest interruption in your texting streak occurs. However, research conducted at Pace University and presented by the American Psychological Association has shown that the way you text might be even more important than the frequency. Couples who text in a similar manner have reported greater relationship satisfaction.

Another issue with texting is that it sometimes affects avoidant behavior. For instance, avoiding a serious but uncomfortable discussion by bringing up one's phone is a common crutch. Instead of texting to avoid problems, you could perhaps use it as an opening for some of the conversations you need to have with your partner. If it's too difficult to say something, getting started over text and then picking it up from there could be very helpful. People used to do it with letters, so there is no reason it couldn't work via text.

Texting and social media may take away from the work that will help the relationship and communication flourish.

https://www.pexels.com/photo/round-table-and-white-table-cloth-3692887/

Social media and how couples behave on it have severe effects on relationships. Often, problems arise when someone takes issue with something their partner has posted. As a rule of thumb, ask yourself how you would feel if your partner posted something before making your own post. Furthermore, while you need personal boundaries, hiding your social media activity from your partner is never a good idea.

Communication Style Quiz

You've already learned some basic ways of assessing your and your partner's communication style, particularly via a checklist of habits, behaviors, and cues. However, individuals can have a million unique ways to communicate, so be as thorough as possible when identifying issues.

More detailed assessments can be very helpful in this regard, such as quizzes that will pose questions about how you communicate in specific situations. Below, you will find several useful questions that can help steer you toward learning more about how you and your partner communicate and where the issues might be, focusing on a few common situations that might occur in most relationships.

You've come home tired and have found that your partner hasn't finished a chore that was their responsibility. How do you react?

1. You reluctantly take care of the chore yourself and say nothing, dwelling on your annoyance.

2. You tell your partner that you've had a really long day and that you'd appreciate it if they would hold up their end of the deal when it comes to chores.

3. You start a fuss and attack your partner for not contributing enough while also throwing in a character attack, such as an accusation of laziness.

How do you deal with criticizing your partner about a mistake they've made?

1. The mistake annoys you, but you're afraid of being too critical and provoking an argument, so you let it slide.

2. You sit down for a comfortable evening with your significant other and casually ease into the conversation, voicing your concerns calmly and rationally.

3. You impulsively react to the mistake or bring it up randomly, perhaps as a weapon to use in an unrelated argument.

What's your usual reaction to financial disagreements, and how do you voice concerns about expenses?

1. You don't want to fight over money, so you say it's alright and move on, even though you're very worried about the impact on your budget.

2. You calmly raise your concern by asking your partner what they think and then state your case.

3. You call them irresponsible and immature.

What do you do when you have expectations and hopes for an upcoming anniversary or birthday?

1. You don't want to be a burden, so you say nothing and pray they'll meet your expectations.

2. You bring it up casually at a leisurely moment and drop a few clever hints.

3. You say nothing because you expect them to read your mind, but then you react with hostility if your expectations aren't met.

You want intimacy at a given moment, so you get your partner's attention in one of three ways.

1. You give them a few ambiguous hints or try to set the mood somehow, but you voice no intentions.
2. You gently move things in that direction and ask if your partner is in the mood.
3. You assume your partner is in the mood whenever you are, so you just grab them.

How do you communicate with your partner regarding your boundaries and alone time?

1. You are worried they might get jealous or feel unwanted, so you put up with too much control, eventually feeling trapped.
2. You explain to your partner that you sometimes need time for yourself and clarify what that entails.
3. You call them needy and shout at them to leave you alone.

One way to differentiate between various communication styles is to categorize them into three kinds. The first is the passive communication style, which is usually characterized by an aversion to conflict and reluctance to voice your opinions and concerns for fear of provoking a confrontation. This communication style leaves things unsaid and can lead to stonewalling, and it corresponds to the answers under number one in the above quiz. Answers under number two signify an assertive communication style. This is the optimal style because it allows for open communication and comfortable expression without aggression. Number three is the aggressive style, which carries all too familiar problems.

Role-reversal and Conflict Resolution Exercises

Last but not least, a simple yet effective empathy exercise is to reverse roles with your partner, at least in your head, when trying to understand their point of view. In relationships where one partner is the breadwinner, for instance, misunderstandings can often happen because the roles in the relationship are so different. If you or your partner can't understand why the other side feels a certain way, you should try your best to imagine yourself in their shoes.

There will be more details on cultivating empathy later in this book, but suffice it to say that role reversal can strengthen communication quite a bit. If the issue is with something simpler than earning a living, you can try to actually reverse roles for a while to see what insights you might get from the experience.

You can also do something similar in terms of conflict resolution. If you have a recurring conflict that keeps popping up, you can create an exercise around reenacting it. This is helpful because it can give you a level-headed perspective on what happens but without the actual drama. You can ask each other questions about what comes next after a typical action or statement and then try to understand why. It's likely that you'll see how silly some of the conflicts are because when you act it out, you will act as a kind of outside observer to your own problems.

Section 5: Resolving Past Issues

As previously hinted in this book, past issues in and outside your relationship can be a massive stumbling block in the way of communication, trust, empathy, and even love itself. These issues cover a wide spectrum of personal experiences that might transpire during your relationship, but they also include an infinite range of personal problems that you and your partner might have brought into the relationship.

Issues from the past that are unresolved can put a lot of negative pressure on your relationship.
https://www.pexels.com/photo/photo-of-a-woman-crouching-while-her-hands-are-on-her-head-5542968/

Past issues, no matter how bad they are, are no reason to despair, especially if they originate from experiences before you two met. When two people come together into a special romantic bond, they bring their entire beings and life stories into the mix. This is natural, and it's a good thing. The problems arise when unaddressed issues are allowed to fester somewhere under the surface until they grow to massive proportions. This section will teach you about past baggage and how to do your best to unburden yourself and your relationship.

The Impact of Past Problems and How to Isolate Them

To understand how the weight of the past can impact relationships, perhaps it is best to break these problems down into three main categories. Personal problems that have nothing to do with relationships, such as trauma, bad experiences from previous relationships, and long-term problems within the current relationship, can all manifest in a number of ways. Many methods for resolving these issues stand true across the categories, but problems need to be identified and understood before they are attempted to be solved.

These problems need to be acknowledged, identified, and addressed because they have a way of weighing down on a relationship and chipping away at it over time. They can lead to chronic tensions and impede your relationship's growth. This is mostly because obstacles will create insecurities and no-go areas regarding topics that can be discussed comfortably. Suppose a certain elephant in the room always produces instability whenever it's brought up. In that case, the foundations of the relationship can't be as stable as they need to be.

Generally, nothing should be left unresolved between two people who share their entire lives. Resolving such problems can be a delicate process, but with patience, communication, trust, and sometimes perhaps a bit of outside help, there's hardly anything you can't manage.

Personal Problems

When it comes to things like trauma, relationships aren't the only aspect of life that will be impacted. Whether it originates in childhood or later on in life, trauma will leave its imprint on the way a person thinks and articulates their emotions, as well as their overall behavior. It often produces problems with one's self-image, leading to negative outlooks on life, other people, and relationships. It's also important not to associate past trauma solely with extreme matters like childhood abuse. Trauma comes in all forms and can be traced to anything from experiences with abuse to bullying, social rejection, and others that can leave a lasting emotional scar on a person.

Signs that past trauma might be affecting your relationship include avoidance of certain topics and activities. This happens because things can come up that remind people of something bad that has happened, and there can be many triggers. That's why trauma makes it difficult to enjoy quality time with one's partner, sometimes in unexpected situations. Reacting with fear, anxiety, defensiveness, irritability, and various other negative emotions in situations where it doesn't make sense are all additional signs of trauma.

Past trauma also leads to disconnection, mistrust, and an overall problem with intimacy through no fault of the affected individual's romantic partner. Whatever difficult experiences you or your partner might have had, the residual effects can be overcome if you manage to get through to each other.

The Residue of Past Relationships

Long-term emotional baggage can also have to do with past relationships. There is a huge spectrum of things that can go wrong in a relationship, so people enter a new relationship with all sorts of negative past experiences. Abusive relationships, experiences with infidelity, a tough breakup, or a tragic loss of one's partner are some things that happen and leave a lasting scar on a person's love life.

While many issues can affect your relationship very similarly to past trauma, baggage from past relationships is much easier to talk about. Unless there was a particularly tragic episode or severe abuse involved, most people would be able to open up relatively easily in a safe space and talk about what they have experienced in a problematic past relationship. However, when they talk too much and too often about their ex, that's usually a sign that people are struggling to get over a past relationship. It doesn't necessarily mean they are still in love with their partner, miss them, or want to get back together. More often than not, it's simply emotional damage due to a failed relationship that hasn't been processed properly.

Hard breakups are probably the most common reason why people struggle to overcome their past relationships, as opposed to extreme cases such as abuse or tragedy. Emotional baggage can leave a person with self-esteem issues, feelings of personal failure, a loss of hope, and a reluctance to truly open up to the prospect of happiness in a new relationship.

Past Burdens Within Your Relationship

Long-standing issues that drag on for years in a relationship result from unaddressed problems that are ignored for one reason or another. This goes back to what you've learned about communication, trust, and intimacy. Whenever you and your partner have a concern that you choose to sweep under the rug to avoid a discussion or because you're feeling insecure, you risk laying the foundations for chronic conflict. This is a very unfortunate state of affairs because, more often than not, these things can be resolved through conversation.

Of course, past transgressions are also the source of long-term resentment and tensions. If the relationship survives, couples will sometimes appear to move on from past dishonesty, infidelity, and similar slights, but the healing process isn't always complete. These issues require thorough processing and must be dealt with openly and thoroughly to be truly resolved. For instance, superficially forgiving mistakes without rebuilding trust is a flimsy foundation on which to build the relationship's future.

Letting Go of the Weight

Everything you've learned in the previous chapters can play a role in resolving past issues with your partner. To open up about these problems (especially deeply rooted personal issues like trauma) requires trust. Even arriving at the topic requires intimacy. Knowing how to resolve conflicts will help minimize the destructive effects of past problems while you work to resolve them. The most important prerequisite, of course, is communication, without which none of these things are possible.

Signs of Trouble

It's always a good first step to ensure that past problems are the real issue troubling your relationship. People can have problems and still function relatively well in relationships, with other areas of the relationship being higher priorities to fix. There are signs to look out for when determining if the main problem lies in your relationship's past.

A common symptom is when a certain problem or topic repeatedly arises during an argument. It can also linger around in normal interactions without necessarily provoking a major argument. Snarky remarks, constantly bringing up the past, taking jabs at each other, and being judgmental about a specific thing from the past are signs of unresolved issues between you and your partner. People who've gotten over past problems might sometimes joke about the past, and this is healthy if it's sincerely just poking fun. However, if there are any hostile undertones, an individual is likely bothered by something.

It will be relatively easy to notice if a past relationship interferes with your current one. Mistrust and communication problems are common symptoms, but the treatment of the current relationship can also be quite telling. Sometimes, people will enter a relationship as an attempt to get over a previous one, and this often happens on a subconscious level. They'll often assume things about you incorrectly and find it difficult to accept that relationships will naturally run into problems. They will create patterns that remind them of their previous relationship, and any current hiccups will lead to frustration instead of a genuine desire to fix it. This is because, for these individuals, the new relationship is a coping mechanism, and they expect it to fix all of their problems.

Getting over Past Transgressions

What you should understand first and foremost is that all relationships will eventually run into some kind of problem and that all of your feelings have validity. Just like topics of discussion, emotions should not be made taboo. If your partner has done something to hurt you or betray your trust in the past, it's natural to feel disappointment or anger with them. It's normal to even reconsider the entire relationship. Still, once you allow yourself to feel your own emotions with sincerity, you'll open the door to the realization that this doesn't have to be the end.

The longer you bury the past, the more internal unresolved issues you will have that will reflect on your relationship.

It's impossible to reconcile with things that you intentionally bury. Think about when you might have been in a fight with a friend, coworker, or someone else to a point where you are no longer on speaking terms. If you've had these experiences and managed to resolve the problem, then you know reconciliation only came after you started talking again. On the other hand, living with someone you care about and continuing to communicate without addressing a serious issue is even less productive than breaking off contact.

When people get angry with each other and cease interacting, they at least know where they stand. The problem is obvious, and the breakdown is over, so it's easier to know what should be done if the relationship is to be healed. Pretending that everything is fine eliminates clarity, muddies the waters, and makes the situation much more difficult to handle.

Anger and disappointment can be addressed and prevented from becoming unbearable resentment over time. When you clearly communicate your feelings to your partner, they are more likely to understand the full impact of their actions, which will motivate them to correct their wrongs or at least ask you what they can do to correct them. Like relationships, people are likely to be imperfect and naturally make mistakes. The trick is to accept and work with them because, at the end of the day, there are all those reasons why you care about them and your relationship.

Forgiveness

That's where forgiveness comes into play. Some people find forgiveness more difficult than others, but everyone can do it for the right person. The important thing is for forgiveness to be genuine, but often, it's possible to think that you've forgiven your partner without truly getting over it, resulting in prolonged bitterness and instability. The way to avoid this is by being honest about your feelings, with yourself first and foremost. This is why valuing your emotions and being open about them is necessary.

Instead of just saying it's fine and rushing to move on to another topic, you should always try to elaborate on your forgiveness and what it really entails. Articulate exactly what troubles you, why you're forgiving your partner, and how you would like to proceed. These words can be more impactful when externalized by being written down, so it's a good idea to write something like a forgiveness letter, which you can try in the space below. If you just need to articulate your feelings, you might choose to keep the letter to yourself, but if you decide to give it to your partner, it can be a great conversation starter.

Reversing Roles via the Empty Chair Technique

As always, reversing roles with your partner and role-playing to study past conflicts can be a great exercise to strengthen your empathy for each other. You might want to explore some aspects of Gestalt therapy, such as the so-called empty chair technique. Gestalt therapy is a holistic approach that focuses on helping individuals gain better insight into themselves, emphasizing their environment, experiences, and relationships. The idea is for patients to understand why they're doing certain things and what they can do to change while also finding inner peace through self-acceptance.

The empty chair technique is all about tackling unresolved feelings and conflicts. The exercise is carried out by instructing an individual to have an imaginary talk with someone by imagining that they are sitting in the empty chair in front of them. Similarly to writing a forgiveness letter, this technique externalizes your inner conflicts and unaddressed feelings you need to articulate. In some sessions, patients might also be instructed to have a conversation with a part of their own personality.

The Empty Chair Technique is a monologue imagined as a dialogue.
https://www.pexels.com/photo/filled-white-coffee-cup-on-saucer-264698/

This is essentially a monologue imagined as a dialogue, and the goal is to talk as clearly and openly as possible to the "person" you're in conflict with. The technique is especially helpful as a precursor if you're still struggling to have a real open conversation with your partner. Simply sit in front of an empty chair, imagine your partner or a part of yourself struggling with past grief, and try to explain your emotions, thoughts, and the way you see your current predicament in as much detail as possible.

After you've stated your case, you can sit in the empty chair, doing your best to respond to what you have just said. These exercises are usually done in the presence of a therapist, but they can also be very helpful on your own. It's a good idea to get a notebook, write down a few bullet points of what you've said before switching chairs, and then address the list from the other side. If you do this enough times, you might be surprised by how much you'll learn about both perspectives just by externalizing your problems verbally.

Stronger Together

Whatever past weight you and your significant other might carry, working together is the only way to unburden your relationship. Depending on your problem, it might require a lot of patience, understanding, and diligent emotional work. As intimate and committed as people in love might be, it's also true that not everyone is equipped with the skills needed to address some of those particularly big personal problems. Sometimes, a bit of outside assistance is just what a couple needs to start moving in the right direction. However, so much can still be done if you and your partner understand each other's needs.

Dealing with Personal Problems

If you and your partner are going to work on a deep, personal problem from the past by yourselves, the healing might take a lot of effort and become an arduous process. When someone struggles with past trauma, it's rarely going to be enough to just sit down for one conversation. You need to create a safe space within your relationship where there will be no judgment and negativity.

You can do this by establishing a set of shared activities you both enjoy, focusing on making them therapeutic and as comfortable as possible. The greatest work, however, will be in applying everything you've learned in the previous sections about building trust and intimacy and improving your communication. Improving any of these aspects of your relationship will make the struggling spouse/partner more comfortable and secure.

It's not always a good idea to jump right into the most difficult conversations and open up all the wounds at once. Facing problems head-on and tackling the full extent of the pain immediately works for some people. Still, it can be incredibly difficult or even counterproductive for others. You should consider an approach similar to what you'll find in exposure therapy, which is often used to treat phobias. Exposing yourself or your partner to painful conversations in small bits, incrementally increasing in severity, can help retain a semblance of comfort while opening up. The idea is to gradually build up tolerance and garner strength to explore further.

Gratitude and Trust

Gratitude is an invaluable aspect of healing from any setbacks in life, and it includes the gratitude you and your partner feel toward each other, as well as being thankful for everything good in your lives overall. You should incorporate gratitude into how you communicate with your partner regularly, always trying to focus on the positives. This will help both of you feel more appreciated and validated while also reminding you how far you've come and why your relationship is so valuable despite what might have happened in the past. Contrast is powerful, and focusing on what's good can help put problems into perspective, making them seem less intimidating.

The importance of trust can also never be overstated. Without trust, it can be impossible to truly move on from past mistakes. It's impossible to open up, making it difficult to address personal problems or talk about the issues. The more you work on trust, the more doors will open between you and your partner, and you'll find that more and more pieces will spontaneously start coming together.

Seeking Professional Help

Dealing with the past and truly moving on from it can be seen as an endeavor combining the things you've learned about in this book thus far. Building trust, nurturing intimacy, communicating openly, and constructively navigating your conflicts will help you tackle any problems that life throws at your relationship, let alone problems that have occurred in the past.

However, a troubled past can also damage a person's mental health. If necessary, you and your significant other should sit down and discuss whether it's time to seek outside counsel. Therapy is a great step toward recovery, and preparing for it by covering the topic extensively with your partner will help you get the most out of it if you decide to go in that direction.

Section 6: Individuality – Why It Matters

The difference between individuality and collectivism is one of the oldest dichotomies of the human experience, or at least it's presented as such. These two aspects of human social behavior don't necessarily have to be at odds. Even though it might seem counterintuitive at first, since relationships entail two people coming together and connecting, individuality actually plays a prominent role in relationships. This section will explore the concept of individuality in more detail, particularly concerning its place within romantic relationships and how to make the most of it to achieve balance between yourself and your partner.

Individuality is something that will add to the value and strength of your relationship.
https://www.pexels.com/photo/young-woman-painting-on-paper-at-workplace-3771055/

False Dichotomies and the Importance of Individuality in Relationships

If you've ever felt like individuality and togetherness are at odds with each other, try to consider what brought you and your partner together in the first place. However it happened, you certainly didn't bump into each other in the street and agree to relinquish your identities and morph into a collective mind! On the contrary, you clicked because you saw certain things you liked about each other.

You can define individuality in a few ways – *but understand that it has nothing to do with selfishness or egocentricity.* The simplest and most common definition says that individuality relates to the qualities and character of a person, particularly in the sense that these things distinguish them from other people. So, individuality is simply about the things that make you unique as a person, no matter how small and seemingly insignificant those things are. It just means you're different, not necessarily separate, and certainly not isolated.

A healthy sense of individuality enables a person to maintain an awareness of their unique qualities and traits without making them feel alienated, interfering with their ability to connect, or causing them to shun the idea of belonging to a team or a community. Your individuality includes all those things you bring to the table when you enter a relationship, and those things are usually what attracts someone to you in the first place.

Individuality is one of the main ingredients in making relationships fulfilling, dynamic, and satisfying. People who hold onto their individuality will maintain their personal identity and all the good things it includes. As such, relationships where individuality is preserved and cherished will enable the couple to enjoy much more of each other. Relationships require more than just two people who make every effort to be copies of each other in order to be dynamic and fulfilling. One of the reasons two people in love can interact so vibrantly is that they have all those small differences, quirks, and thoughts that they find attractive about each other. Of course, many relationships are built on shared interests, and a sense of connection comes from things two people have in common, but the new things they discover about each other along the way are the finest spice.

It's such a major and possibly destructive misconception that partners must share every interest and perspective. While there is some truth in that, many people have found the opposite to be true, which is why popular wisdom also suggests that opposites attract. Your partner is someone you can learn from and who can help you grow as a person, which are some of the most valuable benefits of getting involved in an intimate relationship in the first place.

The key takeaway here is that individuality defines your character's uniqueness and your willingness to maintain that identity. It means being different and being who you are, not being separate or selfish. Even the most consolidated collectives can be made up of people who are strong individuals, and relationships are no exception. Despite common misconceptions, being in a relationship does not require sacrificing your identity and molding yourself into a perfect image that you think is expected of you, nor will this even benefit the relationship.

Relationships entail compromises, of course, but those compromises work best when they are agreed upon by two people who respect each other and are open about what they feel and think. There is thus no mutual exclusivity or contradiction between individuality and collectivism, especially not in relationships. However, striking a fine balance between the two is the key to a healthy relationship. On the extreme ends of this spectrum, individuality can certainly lead to selfishness or egocentrism, while eliminating individuality can lead to dissatisfaction, emotional suffocation, and feelings of being controlled and stripped of your identity.

For a relationship to remain stable, it's crucial that both partners feel affirmed and validated. This means feeling that you are being supported in your efforts and encouraged to be the person you are instead of being judged, controlled, and reshaped in someone else's image. Individuality in relationships has much to do with mutual respect, which comes naturally for most people when they love someone. Unfortunately, personal insecurities sometimes cause people to be more controlling and distrustful of their partner.

None of this is to say that people who are in relationships should always remain completely unchanged over the years. Individuality is more than holding on to every single trait you have and never making a compromise. There is a big difference between controlling someone and encouraging them to improve and achieve their full potential. Healthy relationships tend to gradually move people toward changing for the better, which primarily entails self-improvement.

A supportive partner who truly understands you will awaken your desire to improve yourself and your life, which means building something good on a foundation already there. That foundation is the essence of your identity and what constitutes your individuality. Your essence is what your partner falls in love with, so their respect for who you are comes spontaneously. Their attempts to motivate you to better yourself aren't an infringement on your individuality or an attempt to control you but rather an attempt to keep your spark untarnished.

This positive influence amounts to supportiveness, but the line can sometimes get blurry. This usually happens when there is a communication breakdown, and you fail to clarify boundaries and express your needs. That's how communication plays an integral part in balancing individuality and togetherness. Your partner must understand which parts of your identity you want to cherish and which problems are keeping you down. Only then can they help you become a better version of yourself instead of abandoning your identity.

Balance and the Benefits Gained from Individuality in Relationships

The benefits of individuality in your relationship are more important than you might think. A relationship between two people who respect each other's individuality will certainly be more stimulating, but it's about much more than just excitement and fun.

The fact that partners in a romantic relationship can help each other grow and reach their potential, for instance, is why individuality should not be dismissed. Hobbies are a very good example of this because of their potential. Suppose you require your partner to forego the hobbies they are passionate about. In that case, they won't just become more dissatisfied with their lives. Hobbies that people are passionate about are fulfilling, but they also have the potential to grow and develop into incredible careers, and they offer many other opportunities. If you demand that your partner relinquish this aspect of their individuality, you will directly stifle their potential for personal growth.

Working on your individual strengths can actually bring you closer together.
https://www.pexels.com/photo/photo-of-two-people-using-their-gadgets-1065137/

As people grow toward their true potential, they also bring more to the relationship. Their passion and happiness will reflect on their partner, and they will become more confident, content, and self-aware. All those things learned along the way make each person's journey so inspiring! The new knowledge, skills, and perspectives they'll pick up along that road will be invaluable to their relationships.

People who maintain their identity and are allowed to blossom to the best of their abilities will naturally be better at communicating. They will know themselves and possess a certain inner peace that stems from confidence and fulfillment. This is the stuff that healthy relationships are made of, and individuality plays a decisive role in making that possible.

Individuality is also one of the ingredients in independence and self-reliance. Being overly dependent on each other is a common pitfall for couples in romantic relationships, and it happens as a result of too much control and too many compromises on what makes you who you are. A loving relationship is all about support and sharing, not control and domination.

The Balancing Act

Having a healthy relationship is, in many ways, a balancing act. One of the clearest examples is positioning yourself in that golden middle between maintaining your individuality and making contributions and sacrifices to your relationship. If you truly internalize the idea that you should encourage your partner's personal growth and get the same support in return, you will quickly understand a vital aspect of achieving that balance.

In practical terms, it's setting basic personal boundaries, respecting each other's need for personal space and autonomy, and encouraging the pursuit of each other's hobbies and long-term goals in life. A simple mental exercise for people who share their lives with a significant other is to see it as having two identities. One identity is who you are as a person, which includes your character but also your passions and goals, while the other identity is the couple.

This simple dichotomy will help you understand what you need to do to maintain your identity while doing what is necessary to make your relationship work. To understand where your identity begins and the couple's ends and what your personal boundaries should be, ask yourself simple questions about who you are. Central questions are what you find important, which thoughts and feelings you are unwilling to relinquish, what your values are, which friendships you hold dear, what you need in life, and which interests or hobbies you don't want to give up.

Not being able to answer these questions leads people to relinquish their individuality and become overly dependent on their partner. Once you know who you are and where you are going, you will have a clear outline of what makes you who you are, and you will find that a loving, supportive partner will respect that. The ultimate goal is to balance these things with the knowledge you've learned in the previous sections, such as trust, openness, intimacy, and the common long-term goals of your relationship.

Cherishing Individuality in Your Relationship

Now that you understand how individuality plays into romantic relationships, you can see its potential to make your shared life more fulfilling. There are numerous ways individuality might fit into your particular relationship since every couple is unique in some ways. How you and your partner or spouse incorporate individuality into your lives depends on your characters, needs, expectations, and countless other personal factors that only you will know. Some couples will naturally express less individuality because they might not need it as much. Still, everyone can try a few things to see the positive effects individuality can have on their relationships. The following tips and exercises will help you strengthen the role of individuality between you and your partner.

Setting Goals

Since personal goals are a crucial aspect of your individuality and that of your partner, this is an area where you can practice respecting each other's individuality and becoming more comfortable with it. Partners in a healthy relationship should already have a clear idea of their needs and goals. That's why it's relatively easy for them to set personal goals that don't interfere with the needs of their partnership. A couple should use communication to establish their expectations and what their relationship needs to function and flourish. They can encourage each other to set personal goals when proper communication and trust are established.

You and your partner should have open discussions about what personal goals you might want to set for each other. At the same time, you should also discuss how you can support each other in achieving those goals. With a strong support system, personal goals might even take on the form of a joint endeavor. Encouraging and helping each other to achieve those goals is one of the highest statements of balance between individuality and togetherness.

This is why support for personal undertakings and ambition feels so validating. It strengthens the feeling of appreciation and respect while also reinforcing trust. Relationships are also about guidance, so this doesn't mean giving unconditional support without input to every idea one of you has. Through honest discussions, however, it's always possible to smooth things out and figure out the best course.

You can always support the goal while having a few things to say about the proposed road toward that goal. For example, suppose your partner wants to change career paths or become an entrepreneur. In that case, this goal is definitely worthy of support. However, if they want to quit their job immediately without setting a new path for themselves, it may or may not be a good idea. It is important to discuss it and ensure your partner's personal goals are taken seriously and encouraged.

Allocating Personal Space

Most people will need at least a bit of personal space at some point, and this is another common expression of individuality. There are activities that some people enjoy and get the most out of only when they're on their own, which is natural. There are also those thoughts and feelings that are sometimes best resolved through some good old-fashioned soul-searching. At first glance, it might seem difficult to differentiate between a plain need for personal space and a communication problem. If your partner wants to do something independently, you might misconstrue that as stonewalling or avoidance. However, these misunderstandings will only happen if there are insecurities and poor communication in your relationship *to begin with.*

If you are patient and open-minded, it will be easy to discuss these things with your partner and realize that their need for some personal space doesn't mean something is wrong between you. It's also beneficial to create a personal space plan together by agreeing on separate times for being alone; this will help avoid co-dependency. This course is good if you're simultaneously resolving your communication issues and building trust. If you sit down and make a schedule that allocates and clearly defines personal space, there will be no surprises and uncomfortable moments that need explaining. Spontaneity has its own charms, of course, but for struggling couples, it's best to keep it within the confines of shared activities and quality time you spend together.

Exploring Interests

You can also encourage each other to explore new interests and activities to introduce more individuality into the relationship. Sometimes, you or your partner might feel like you've been neglecting your individuality simply due to a lack of effort, not necessarily because you have been trying to control the other. This can lead to just as much dissatisfaction with life, which also reflects on the relationship.

Sometimes, it's necessary to give your partner a push to encourage and cherish each other's individuality. This joint exercise could bring quite a bit of novelty and excitement into your lives. For instance, you can sit down and talk to each other about what kinds of new hobbies, interests, and activities you might be interested in but have never tried. You should engage in these activities independently and in your own personal time. After you try these new hobbies, you can share your experiences with each other.

These novelties can produce interesting conversations, and you might also learn new things about each other. It could be that you or your partner used to consider individuality as something unwanted or detrimental to your relationship, so you never brought up certain interests you would have liked to explore. Once you understand that personal pursuits can fit into a relationship, you might find yourselves unlocking new and exciting areas in your lives.

Getting excited about new things, enjoying some freedom, and then returning home to share your excitement and passion could be a very rejuvenating experience for your relationship. When creating a list or discussing these new personal activities, go into some detail on what the activities might entail. More precisely, it's always good to let your partner know what they're in for, particularly if a new hobby requires considerable financial or otherwise investment.

Establishing Boundaries

Finally, it's worth reiterating the importance of personal boundaries in a functional relationship. Communicating about the issue is the simplest and perhaps most important exercise. Unfortunately, the topic of personal boundaries arises only after one of the partners in the relationship starts to feel that theirs has been violated. If you and your partner can talk openly about how you feel, this isn't a major issue because you know you can just sit down and smooth things out.

However, it's best to prevent these feelings from happening in the first place by setting personal boundaries within the relationship ahead of time. When discussing this with your partner, your goal should be to clearly define areas of your life where you truly feel you need to handle things independently. You must differentiate between personal boundaries and the urge to avoid certain topics or activities with your partner. If you have a problem, especially concerning the relationship, your "personal boundary" should never be to keep it to yourself.

Personal boundaries usually concern things that aren't very consequential for your relationship, such as having a private office at home or spending time with a friend. Whatever your boundaries, you should talk about them openly with your partner and identify them as clearly as possible. Your partner should also be given the opportunity to do the same. If you struggle with giving each other personal space and find each other overbearing, you can start with minor steps.

For instance, going to the mall and then separating to run your own errands or do your shopping can be a valuable yet easy exercise. These activities reinforce the idea that you can handle things separately and make your own decisions before returning *home together.*

Section 7: Planning Your Future

The matter of individuality in relationships and the balance between it and togetherness also feeds into what this section will focus on. Every relationship should focus on the future for two main reasons. Firstly, long-term relationships are always built with at least some foresight and consideration for where things might go. People who don't make future considerations when getting romantically involved don't end up in serious and ongoing relationships, either by choice or as a spontaneous consequence of how they live. Secondly, the future, in general, is a major factor in how a relationship develops.

Planning a healthy future together takes communication and compromise.
https://www.pexels.com/photo/cheerful-young-spouses-preparing-for-moving-in-new-apartment-4246182/

So, planning for the future is something that every couple should know how to do. How you make plans and adapt to unforeseen developments can make or break what you've been building in your relationship. This section will explore how your future plays a part in your relationship, how to make plans to ensure that things go smoothly in the future, and a few tips on how to get better at planning in general.

Alignment with Your Partner

Couples tend to have multiple visions for the future, focusing on different aspects of life. For one, everyone has at least a basic vision for their own personal future, no matter how basic of an outline it might be. Everybody has at least a few things they'd like or wouldn't like to see in their lives years later. Then, there are the future expectations that relate specifically to the relationship, which can also be seen as the relationship's needs.

In relationships, aligning your long-term goals with your partner's is paramount. Finding common ground between your shared vision for your relationship's future and your individual dreams and goals is another crucial balancing act you must focus on. Suppose your individual goals don't fit in with what your relationship will require. In that case, it's difficult to maintain stability in the long term. Being too self-centered and putting your needs before the relationship is one of the surest ways of eroding and eventually destroying a relationship. On the other hand, sacrificing too many personal goals can lead to chronic discontent, friction, and even resentment. Both of these extremes are equally detrimental.

Aligning your personal goals and dreams with your partner and relationship is an exercise that can be different from one couple to another. Still, there are a few general rules that you should follow. These mostly involve self-reflection because alignment starts with you and your partner individually. You can't make decisions for each other or tell each other what goals you should pursue, so both of you need to start in your own backyard, so to speak.

The first step in that direction is to take a good look inside yourself and make sure that you know where you're headed in the first place. Being goal-oriented and following a clear path is one of the best recipes for long-term stability overall, which translates into relationships. Nobody can control everything that life throws their way, but main goals can be set well in advance. If you and your partner know each other's passions and dreams, it will be easier to make decisions together while ensuring they are in line with the relationship's goals.

Similarly, it's beneficial to understand your values and core beliefs, especially regarding relationships, while communicating them clearly to your partner. Couples who are clear on their individual values will have an easier time aligning with each other in the long term because it'll be easier to articulate their expectations. For instance, if you're trying to envision a future for your relationship, consider where you stand on things like marriage or having kids.

Some people will maintain a serious, long-term relationship even if they don't want marriage, but that's still a decision they've arrived at by thinking about the future and articulating their personal views on relationships. Knowing exactly what you want and don't want for your relationship will make it possible to keep your partner informed on where you stand. Problems usually emerge when this topic isn't given its due thought and consideration, leaving things ambiguous and strained. Without information, your partner will be left guessing and probably start to unconsciously fill in the blanks. This can build up assumptions or expectations that might catch you off guard when you least expect them, and the sudden realization of mismatched and unsaid expectations is a rather common cause of breakups.

At the end of the day, aligning your individual dreams and goals in the relationship boils down to articulating said goals, transparency, communication, and a bit of compromise. Remember that this alignment is an ongoing process that you'll need to maintain over time. Decisions and new directions, which are certain to come, need to be reviewed and adjusted if needed.

While you and your partner should respect each other's personal goals, every decision for the future should be evaluated within the context of the relationship. When contemplating a plan or any other long-term decision, always ask yourself how it will affect the relationship, how it fits into your shared vision as a couple, and whether it's compatible. There is no reason to reflect on these things silently. The more you consult with your partner and share feedback, the lower the chances of future complications.

During that process, you may run into certain differences. Regardless of how well you get along, you and your significant other will sometimes see certain things differently. However, these differences won't be a major obstacle if they don't relate to the nature of your relationship on a fundamental level. You can disagree on finances, career paths, or where to live, but surface issues are easy to resolve if you're on the same frequency regarding where your relationship is headed and what it means to you.

If you maintain open lines of communication, intimacy, and trust, there are very few disagreements you won't be able to negotiate through as long as you both have the same expectations or at least a clear compromise on how you see your relationship developing over the years.

Working Together

Planning for the future is integral to every healthy and fulfilling relationship. The benefit isn't only in having a clear plan and a secure long-term path, though. Working on these plans together brings couples closer and is one of the best ways to improve the relationship overall. Planning for your future as a couple also has the added effect of putting your relationship in perspective and reminding you of what you're working toward.

Setting goals, in general, is a good way to strengthen a sense of purpose in what you're doing. This is easily felt individually, even when you set small goals only a few days ahead. Having a clear long-term goal in life, however, is a well-known and useful tool for keeping yourself focused and motivated. In that regard, relationships are a lot like individuals. The purpose is indeed easier to find when you're with someone you love, but making plans and talking about all those good things that the two of you want in the future will only strengthen your resolve.

Getting on the Same Page

Joining forces and consulting each other when making future plans will reinforce trust and elevate the confidence that both of you have in the relationship. This is because the very act of talking about your shared future demonstrates to both of you that the other side factors in the relationship when making any decisions for the future. It acknowledges your commitment to the relationship and makes it clear that your relationship is something you both hold dear and have no intention of abandoning.

It takes constant discussions and planning to really see where you want to go together in your future plans.

https://www.pexels.com/photo/young-indian-couple-counting-bills-on-calculator-4308058/

If you've never spent much time discussing the future with your partner, breaking the ice might initially be a little jarring. A common inhibition people have is worrying that they'll come across as needy and incessant toward their partner, possibly pressuring them too much and ultimately driving them away. In healthy relationships, mentioning the future and expressing your expectations is never a problem. This is especially true if the inquiring partner makes sure they ask the other side for their thoughts and feedback, giving room for constructive back-and-forth.

However, if communicating on this level is an issue in your relationship, gradually ease into the topic. You don't necessarily have to jump straight into the traditional "Where do you see us in five years?" type of questions. A good entry point is casually bringing up things like hopes, dreams, ambitions, career goals, and other future paths that your partner might have without referring to your relationship specifically.

When you get your partner talking, encourage them to discuss what they want to do with their life. It won't take long before you can gauge certain hints about how much your relationship factors in for your partner's future planning. Suppose you're already on the same page in terms of emotional investment. In that case, they'll probably bring it up on their own by pointing out how your relationship fits into their plans.

Honesty plays a crucial role in these discussions, as there is no other way for the two of you to ascertain where you stand.

Once the discussion undoubtedly moves on to your relationship's future, you can outline your individual visions. This means doing your best to harmonize your potentially different points of view. The starting point is an agreement that you both care and want to build your relationship in the future, after which you'll determine if adjustments need to be made to your plans.

Individuality and the Power of Support

Your best strategy for harmonizing your visions for the future is extensive communication. You must listen closely to your partner and be honest and open. One of the best ways to foster understanding is to help each other articulate your goals, including career paths, family life, overall lifestyle, and personal growth.

If one of you struggles to articulate personal goals (and no verbal encouragement seems to help), your best bet is to externalize the mental process via paper.

As in previously mentioned exercises, things like lists and simple quizzes can do wonders to make sense of jumbled thoughts. You can start with something very simplistic, such as basic lists of desires in different categories like work, education, lifestyle, and anything relevant.

Once you have listed those desires, you and your partner can determine the practical steps toward fulfillment. When you start getting ideas, you'll find it easy to analyze how those plans will fit your relationship goals. This is the simplest path toward getting you and your partner on the same frequency and helping you decide which compromises to make and when.

As previously discussed, relationships will benefit from preserving the partners' individuality, including future planning. Romantic relationships are a force of nature, but they also make some of the best support systems you can find. Similarly, to the family you come from, especially parents, the support you do or don't get from your partner can affect you as an individual.

Striking the perfect balance between compromises and individual aspirations will enable you to give each other the best support while keeping your relationship stable. As the two of you explore the future and your plans in more and more detail over time, you may find all sorts of unexpected inspirations, interests, and passions. Romantic partners have a way of awakening these things in each other and realizing that someone intimately close to you is there to support you and can be a strong wind on your back.

Practical Planning and Setting Goals

To set up practical long-term goals together as a team, you and your partner will need to communicate about the future consistently and openly. Relationships, where everything is out in the open without inhibition, will have the easiest time adjusting to changes and standing the test of time. This is especially true regarding goals and plans because it ensures no major surprises lead to instability.

Ideally, you and your partner should never end up in a situation where one surprises the other with a major and sudden shift in their life goals, especially a shift that can impact the relationship. When you talk openly about your passions, expectations, dreams, and ideas, it's very unlikely that this will ever happen. Important decisions that can affect the relationship should always be made together, taking input from both sides. Knowing how to plan more effectively and cover all your bases in different areas of life is necessary.

The point to take home is that you and your partner should work in unison whenever possible. Leave room for individuality where you can, but take advantage of the fact that two minds are stronger than one whenever you're considering the growth of your relationship. Your first step should be to identify your priorities as a couple by making a list of goals that you agree on. These goals include everything from buying a car to getting married and having children.

As you would when trying to help each other articulate your personal goals, making common, united goals as a couple can also benefit from the written form. Setting aside a few hours every week to explore this topic in detail during a quiet evening at home with your partner can be helpful. Goals should be as straightforward and comprehensive as possible to make it easier to stay focused.

For instance, they can consist of three properties, including the goal's category, a brief description of the goal itself, and one or more actions to be taken toward that goal. Common categories are finances, professional life, lifestyle, family, health, or personal growth. To articulate these goals with your partner, use a simple goal-setting template like the one below. Perhaps you and your partner have decided to improve your health or fitness. You might open the template with a fitness category and create a corresponding goal, such as running one mile daily. That simple goal can require various actions, such as buying running shoes or finding a suitable area. The same principle applies to more complex, long-term goals. Something else to consider is that united goals can still leave room for individual action. Suppose you and your partner have the common goal of buying a house. Joining forces to achieve that goal means task allocation between you, such as you looking for options and your partner contacting the respective real estate agencies. While buying the house is a common goal, the finer details of the plan are made up of what you might consider to be personal goals for both of you.

While fitness is a convenient example, the above methods can apply to any long-term goals in your relationship. The more you practice planning and goal-setting with your partner on regular, everyday activities, the more natural it'll become for you to make plans together. Communication and intimacy will benefit immensely from these activities, and you might not even realize that you're gradually becoming much more comfortable with each other and the future. It's also guaranteed that any changes and plans you make will be much easier to accomplish with your significant other at your side.

Whatever your goals, to get your priorities right and motivate yourself to stick to the plan, using a vision board might also be a good idea. A vision or dream board is a simple and creative endeavor that usually entails a collage of pictures, other visuals, affirmative messages, and important goals or reminders. It can be a fun, leisurely activity when you and your partner spend your free time together. Your vision board will be unique to your life, but its objective is to inspire and motivate both of you.

You can create a vision board that more broadly refers to your relationship and its goals, or it can consist of something more specific, such as your united journey toward physical fitness or anything else you're working on together. Making a vision board is easy and requires little time or materials. A sizeable bulletin board works perfectly because it provides plenty of space to thoroughly personalize the board with photos, catchphrases, reminders, written priorities, and much else.

Creating a vision board doesn't have to be a one-time exercise. If your board has enough space, things can be added later on. Putting it up at a prominent place in your home creates a shared place of casual expression for you and your partner. It's a collage of ideas where you can put up new plans and a pin in things you'd like to see in the future.

Your vision board can be a way to create pleasant surprises for your partner. For instance, a sudden idea you've had for a vacation spot can go up on the vision board and brighten up your partner's day when they see it. If you have your board up for a long time, it can also become a humble collage of memories and feelings. Thoughts, feelings, and affirmative messages you pin for each other can catch your attention again a couple of years later and be a pleasant reminder of the things that matter.

The most valuable message to internalize is that your plans are only as good as your communication with each other. The more you discuss your plans and explore their finer details with a strong regard for each other's input, the more feasible and consistent your plans will be. There will be less room for mistakes and unpleasant surprises if you and your partner clearly know what the other expects from your plans and why. As long as you are in complete harmony and clarity as to the ultimate goals of your relationship, you will both have an easy time making all the necessary compromises.

Section 8: Cultivating Empathy

In the long term, empathy will be one of the most powerful factors in maintaining and keeping your relationship stable. Empathy is an inherent human trait that has played a crucial role in helping people survive and thrive. More precisely, the ability to organize and communicate on such a uniquely sophisticated level has been the deciding factor in most of the major human accomplishments throughout history. *And a lot of that is thanks to people's ability to empathize with each other.*

Empathy is an ongoing task you must work on with your partner throughout your life.

Empathy's importance cannot be overstated; it makes it possible to understand your partner, communicate effectively, resolve conflicts, and make plans together. When couples can effectively empathize with each other, they can resolve most problems easily. Still, sometimes, *empathy itself is the problematic area that needs attention.* This section will take a deep dive into the concept of empathy, why it matters so much, and what you can do to improve it.

The Definition and Nature of Empathy

In the simplest terms, empathy is all about emotional understanding between people. It allows you to recognize certain emotions in others, whether basic and visible things like fear or something more subtle and complex, like envy. The greater the range of emotions one can recognize in others, the more empathetic they are. Empathy makes it possible to put yourself in someone else's figurative shoes and imagine, as accurately as possible, what they might be going through.

Empathy is an unspoken yet universal human language deeply rooted in evolution. The ideas around empathy have certainly absorbed some societal and cultural influence across different times and spaces, but the underlying ability is biological and has been around for a very long time. The presence of cruelty and all manner of malice in the world certainly poses the question of why empathy sometimes appears to be absent in people, given that it comes so naturally to the majority. Given all these factors, empathy has been studied quite a bit over the years.

Scientific research into empathy goes back more than a hundred years (to 1909) and the work of psychologist Edward B. Titchener. Since then, different scientific disciplines have proposed theories and explanations as to where empathy comes from. In neuroscience, more recent research has shown that certain parts of the human brain are particularly active in relation to empathy, such as the anterior insula and the anterior cingulate cortex.

This research doesn't necessarily explain why humans have empathy, but it makes it quite clear that it's at least partly a neurobiological process. Scans have also shown the involvement of the inferior frontal gyrus in the process of empathy. Further reinforcing the theory of empathy as a natural occurrence is that damage to the IFG can hinder a person's ability to recognize the emotions behind other people's facial expressions and, in turn, connect with them.

Other explanations and theories about empathy are mostly emotional and social. Adam Smith, for instance, theorized that the purpose of empathy was partly to improve people's emotional depth through the experience of feeling the emotions of others. Having such a wide range of emotional experiences, via your own experiences and those of others, would thus serve to train you emotionally. Since people can empathize with real and fictional characters, they can experience many emotions they may not encounter alone.

Viewing empathy through a sociological lens offers a more utilitarian, rational look. According to sociologist Herbert Spencer, humans have developed empathy as an adaptation that has played an important survival role because it facilitates the impulse to help others. Humans have evolved as a very social species, so empathy is right at home in healthy human interactions. Empathy plays a constructive social role in the grand scheme of things and encourages socially beneficial behavior. On the individual level, this means helping out a neighbor or relative in need. On a higher level, it means people coming together to accomplish great feats of civilization.

The definition of empathy usually categorizes it into three main types: affective, somatic, and cognitive empathy. Affective empathy is about emotions, which people usually think about when discussing empathy. It's your ability to understand what someone else is feeling and emotionally react to that. For instance, when your partner's emotional state makes you worry about them, you are experiencing affective empathy. A more pronounced manifestation of this is when their emotional pain causes distress or outright pain for you, as well.

Somatic empathy is interesting because it involves spontaneous physical reactions to what someone else is experiencing. For example, when you witness embarrassment or emotional distress in another person and feel a physical reaction such as blushing, an elevated heart rate, sweating, or an uneasy feeling in your stomach, that's somatic empathy.

Cognitive empathy relates to thoughts and is perhaps the most rational of the three types. You can understand what someone else is thinking without asking but solely based on their situation. Part of this ability is thanks to your own experience and logic; however, it also involves the conscious effort of putting yourself in the other person's shoes and imagining yourself facing that same situation. It's a quick exercise in mental role reversal; for some people, it's partly intuitive.

A distinction should be made between empathy and sympathy. Sympathy is fairly synonymous with compassion, so it definitely bears a fair amount of resemblance to empathy. However, sympathy tends to be passive, stopping short of making a real effort to understand another person, which is the essence of empathy. Feeling bad for someone having a rough time doesn't take a lot of emotional or mental effort. Still, you need empathy to truly understand them and feel what they're feeling. Sympathy can be felt for any random stranger on the street, but your partner (in an intimate relationship) is the person to whom you're connected on a deeper level.

You can fairly accurately assess your level of empathy based on how other people treat you. If they often approach you for advice, consider you a good listener, and confide in you about their problems, you are very likely empathetic. This isn't necessarily something that you and the other person have to discuss. People will simply feel how you empathize and naturally gravitate toward you.

Your own actions and responses are also something you should analyze. On the emotional level, you should consider how you respond to tragic news, how easily you detect deception, and how much you truly care about the problems of others. Deeply empathetic people will sometimes struggle to say no and establish personal boundaries, which is one example of how empathy can go too far. So, you should be careful and considerate with a deeply empathetic partner in a relationship since they will need you to respect them and have their best interest at heart.

Problems and Obstacles

As wonderful as empathy is, it can wreak havoc in your life if it isn't restrained by reason and self-respect. Not keeping your empathy under control can exhaust you and make you feel like the weight of the world is crashing down on you. Being overwhelmed by too much empathy will wear anybody down and lead to exhaustion. People with this problem often feel drained after extensive social interaction, which is the least of the issues that can arise.

These feelings are referred to as empathy fatigue, which is tiresome and can lead to an empathy shutdown overall. Feelings of weakness, isolation, and lethargy are common symptoms, and they can have a severe impact on your social interactions. Think of it like any other system where overexertion leads to a crash. It's particularly dangerous when this happens with empathy because you might become unresponsive or even lose compassion for periods of time. This isn't good for anyone, especially you and people very close to you, such as your partner. To avoid being overwhelmed by empathy, you need to keep things in perspective and stay realistic, employing logic and reason to understand that you can't always help everyone and that emotionally draining yourself will have no positive effects on anyone, least of all yourself.

Empathy fatigue is one of the causes behind a lack of empathy, but it's usually periodic. There are many other reasons people might lack empathy in certain situations or life in general. A lack of empathy often results in antisocial behavior and has a profoundly negative effect on relationships. Significant personality disorders, such as narcissism, can accompany it. However, healthy individuals can also have diminished empathy.

A lack of empathy can result in antisocial behavior.

Common barriers to empathy include cognitive biases, which come in various forms. Having a cognitive bias can make it difficult for you to interpret the world objectively. Having a hard time understanding other people and their feelings is just one of the symptoms of this thinking error. Cognitive biases can sometimes be rather subtle, making them tricky to eliminate. A common cognitive bias that diminishes empathy is the idea that people who go through a rough time can only blame themselves for their circumstances.

When you look at the world through such a lens, it's very hard to empathize with people and their predicaments. Internally, a cognitive bias can result from being too harsh on yourself, thus projecting the same scrutiny onto others. Suppose you have a very low opinion of yourself and always think that everything bad that happens to you is solely your own failure. In that case, you may very well treat the problems of others in the same way. The opposite can also be true since some people will lack compassion when looking at other people's failures while, at the same time, always attributing personal failures to external factors.

All sorts of preconceived notions, distractions, and inclinations toward judgment can also make empathy difficult. Victim blaming is a common problem that diminishes people's empathy. It's a very easy pit to fall into and can creep up on you in the subtlest and most unexpected of ways, as it's not always egregious and can even sound reasonable. Think about a hypothetical scenario involving a tragic traffic accident involving a pedestrian who was jaywalking.

Quite a few people will react to the news by commenting that the pedestrian shouldn't have been jaywalking and that they would still be alive had they obeyed traffic regulations. While this may be very true, it is a statement that serves no practical purpose other than suppressing empathy. The empathetic response would be to acknowledge the tragedy, wonder about the victim's family, or even offer assistance if possible.

The problem with victim blaming is that it can be strangely gratifying, which is why many people do it unconsciously and default to it. Commenting that someone could have avoided their negative outcome demonstrates perceived personal competence, noting that the commentator would have done better or been smarter in a given situation. These statements stroke the ego, but they don't really help anyone or offer any value, least of all to the person making the statement. As you can see, this attitude can easily apply to relationships and is, unfortunately, quite common.

In almost all cases, the antidote is to listen attentively and actively to what other people are telling you, especially your partner. Everything you've learned about empathizing and communicating in the previous sections will help you unblock your mind. Letting go of biases and breaking the habit of preconceptions and conclusion-jumping can sometimes be a significant mental undertaking, but there is a lot you can do to bolster your empathy.

Developing and Cultivating Empathy

Putting aside cases that involve severe mental health issues, deeply entrenched personality disorders, or brain damage, empathy is a skill that you can learn and improve a fair amount. In some ways, it's like a muscle group that you must train with the right exercises – if you want to strengthen it. The overwhelming majority of people can do this with empathy without much trouble. It's usually not difficult, especially when you're in a relationship, but it can sometimes take a while.

Apart from previously discussed methods like active listening, learning the ins and outs of body language can also help bolster your empathy. Reading body language boils down to taking note of your partner's posture, subtle facial expressions, and gestures. These are non-verbal cues that people give off mostly unconsciously, and they can reveal things like openness, comfort, discomfort, anxiety, relaxation, happiness, frustration, and countless other emotions and mental states.

A common worksheet used in individual and group therapy sessions with clients who struggle with empathy entails telling an empathy story. The first step is to choose a certain story, which can be a story about someone you know or something you've read in the paper. After choosing a story, you can choose the medium you want to use to tell it, like writing, video, narration, art, or anything else that applies. It can also be told in person, directly to someone else.

Your significant other would be the ideal partner for this exercise. The point of the exercise is to tell the story in a way that emphasizes how the protagonist felt and why, with an attempt to dissect and understand those emotions. Explain what that person felt and why, then do your best even if you don't find the story relatable. Using a relatable story would work best, but identifying one can be difficult when you struggle with a lack of empathy. Once you tell and analyze the story, you should ask your partner to analyze it similarly and describe the emotions they could identify. You and your partner can both choose and tell these stories, regardless of whether or not empathy is an issue for both of you. In fact, if one partner is more empathetic than the other, the other side could learn quite a lot from them during this exercise.

Something else you and your partner can do is the so-called "What Am I Feeling?" game. The premise is very simple, involving various topics that can be summarized in single words, which will serve as cues. The idea is to pick a topic and then try to guess what your partner is feeling or thinking about. This can be an especially effective exploratory activity for romantic partners because they usually know each other quite well. It can be an entirely verbal game, or you could make cards with different words or topics written on them.

In general, one of the quintessential mental tricks to stimulate your empathy is to train your brain to seek out similarities instead of differences in people. This is such a simple yet incredibly effective mental change that can help you see the world in a very different light if you manage to turn it into a habit. Your brain will spot all the minuscule ways you are different from someone else very easily and often by default.

This is natural, and it's not a problem in and of itself, but the trick is to remember not to make those differences the area of focus when perceiving someone else. Focusing instead on all the similarities you share with others whenever you're out and about will gradually make you more open to seeing who they are and what they are feeling. This is a fundamental change in the thinking process for many people, so there are many daily opportunities to practice it.

Whether the issue is with your partner or people in general, growing your empathy requires daily practice while avoiding the obstacles above. Listen instead of interrupting, ask well-intentioned questions instead of judging, and focus on people's feelings. It sounds simple enough, but it might require a prolonged commitment to get the hang of it. However, seeing as you've made it to a point in your life where you are in a serious relationship, becoming more empathetic is likely a matter of minor attitude adjustments and just talking more with your partner.

Section 9: Vulnerability – Strength through Openness

It should be clear by now that vulnerability in relationships has much to do with trust and intimacy, but it's also a quality of its own. Unfortunately, vulnerability carries a negative connotation in many people's minds, although the aversion is understandable. As emotional creatures prone to all sorts of insecurities and worries, human beings naturally fear being hurt emotionally. Self-preservation is an instinct that all living things possess, but humans are the only beings whose self-preservation instincts go well beyond just preserving physical integrity.

Vulnerability is a quality that disarms your partner and allows them to open up and trust you more.
Photo by Liza Summer: https://www.pexels.com/photo/woman-comforting-desperate-girlfriend-and-embracing-gently-6382530/

For people, emotional damage can be just as, if not more frightening than physical harm. As a consequence, emotional vulnerability in our modern society is discouraged and generally stigmatized, but the real trouble is when vulnerability is falsely equated with weakness. Nobody wants to be seen as weak, and that's completely natural. Still, the truth is that vulnerability doesn't imply weakness and that it has a vital role to play in relationships. This section will explore that idea in more depth and delve into how vulnerability can be encouraged, developed, and put to healthy use in your relationship.

Vulnerability in Relationships

In the context of romantic relationships, vulnerability primarily concerns your ability and readiness to open yourself up emotionally to your partner. As you've seen in previous discussions, opening up to your partner and having that openness reciprocated is half the battle. It's impossible to build trust with your partner without being open, and it's even less likely that you'll be able to strengthen emotional or even physical intimacy when you shut them out.

Vulnerability and trust are so closely intertwined because the decision to truly open yourself up to another person carries inherent risks – or at least perceived risks. It's somewhat of a chicken and egg dilemma, too, since allowing yourself to be vulnerable enables you to build up trust, while trust makes it easier to be vulnerable. These two crucial aspects of your relationship feed into each other, are strongly correlated, and must be nurtured equally.

Showing your true feelings and vulnerability also entails letting the other person in on your weaknesses, which everyone has. This is one of the reasons many people wrongfully treat vulnerability and weakness as synonymous. While showing your weaknesses to the entire world is not the most sustainable strategy, it works differently in intimate relationships. Your partner should know and be mindful of your weaknesses if they explain and understand where you're coming from and empathize with you more deeply.

Without understanding and empathy, relationships will never reach that deeper level and become as strong as you need them to be. This is how vulnerability becomes a source of strength. It initially strengthens the relationship by bringing a couple closer and developing their bond. Since being in a healthy relationship with someone who supports and understands you without judgment can change your entire life, vulnerability also strengthens the individual.

Think about all those personal problems that people might have, which they keep hidden and suppressed out of fear. More often than not, letting the right person in is exactly what's needed to tackle those problems and begin healing. Unaddressed, these issues will only worsen over the years, making functioning in relationships and life difficult. This is how misguided attempts to project an image of strength by closing yourself off from the world lead to real weakness.

The fear of judgment is why many people avoid being vulnerable. It's especially unfortunate when this fear is vindicated by opening up to the wrong person and getting hurt, which can certainly happen. If you've had an experience like that, it's understandable if you're reluctant to allow yourself to be vulnerable. Nonetheless, you should look at it through the prism of risk and reward, understanding that the reward of opening up to the right person is well worth the emotional risk.

One of the underappreciated benefits of vulnerability is that it can promote personal growth. It's not just about revealing your problems or weaknesses and allowing your partner to help you overcome them. Openness means letting another person in on all your hopes and dreams in life, even those you are insecure about because you might feel they are silly or unrealistic.

It's not uncommon for people to convince themselves that a certain goal or dream they have is unrealistic or even worthy of ridicule. Goals can certainly be objectively too lofty, but few things are impossible to accomplish with enough work, dedication, and motivation. Sometimes, the support and guidance of someone you trust might be just the boost you need to unlock your true potential.

The bottom line with vulnerability in relationships is that it's simply necessary. Without it, there can be no deeper understanding, no true empathy, and no way for your partner to see things from your perspective. This pitfall can ruin most relationships because feeling understood and truly known is one thing that draws people to relationships in the first place. Not being understood is a fairly common reason that people cite when explaining why their relationship feels emotionally unsatisfying or why it ended.

Some folks don't realize that being understood isn't something they should leave entirely to their partner and just expect it by default. It takes effort on both sides, which mostly boils down to opening up. You can consider this in a very practical sense, as well. In healthy relationships, partners will understand each other's needs, desires, expectations, and boundaries well. When people in a relationship aren't open with each other and constantly close off due to their inhibitions, it will be very difficult to communicate their expectations and outlook on the relationship overall.

These barriers will inevitably lead to conflict, dissatisfaction, unmet needs, disappointment, and much more detrimental to a relationship's prospects. If you need your partner to understand you and meet your expectations, you shouldn't make it more difficult for them. They can be the most empathetic person in the world, but if you hold on to your fear of letting them in and are continuously shutting them off, there will be little they can do to get through to you. Thus, working on your vulnerability or helping your partner work on theirs is sometimes the first step needed to strengthen your relationship.

Encouraging Vulnerability in Your Relationship

The first step toward making vulnerability less taboo is simply talking about it. A thorough discussion about the concept of vulnerability, how it might fit into your relationship, and what it means to you and your partner can be just the thing to get the ball rolling. Let your partner know how vulnerability makes you feel while also making sure they express their feelings about it.

You need to tell each other what the act of vulnerability makes you feel.
https://www.pexels.com/photo/crying-helpless-black-woman-sitting-on-windowsill-6382589/

People who have an aversion toward vulnerability can react to it in different ways. Some will feel anxious, others will get moderately depressed, and some will react with anger. Furthermore, what people feel isn't always what they express clearly. When feeling vulnerable, your partner might visibly react by going quiet while, under the surface, they are experiencing intense anger. Whatever the case is with you or your partner, to be fully understood, these emotions must be discussed, as they might require different approaches.

Past experiences with vulnerability are also a valuable topic to explore. However, personal history can be one of the more difficult topics to take up. Suppose you or your partner can explain when and how you were hurt in the past, especially before your relationship. In that case, you might gain quality insight into ways to help each other feel more comfortable and trusting.

You must lead by example, especially if only one of you is struggling. It's not enough to tell your partner they should be more open and less fearful of vulnerability. No matter how well you frame it and how rational of a case you state for openness, you still have to practice what you preach. You should show your partner that neither of you should have anything to fear and that you feel perfectly comfortable sharing your thoughts, feelings, and fears with them. Ensure they can see how much they help you when they listen and understand your concerns. It will make them feel good to know that you are relying on them.

This is a strong motivator for them to reciprocate and start opening up more to you. It's about promoting a sense of security in your relationship and creating a space of safety and empathy. It's also not enough to simply trust your partner without accounting for why they might have trouble doing the same. You must always do your best to be trustworthy and reliable, not just by being honest but also by leaving no room for them to doubt you. Don't leave things unsaid and unaddressed because that's how you create room for their thoughts to feed on their insecurities.

Trust can be very fragile for people struggling with vulnerability, so you must start small and be careful. Even in the most mundane and seemingly unimportant situations, demonstrating your openness and trustworthiness can go a long way toward making your partner more relaxed. If you have to crawl before walking, so be it, but you're likely to be surprised by how fast you can create a more comfortable environment if you make the right adjustments. The most important thing in terms of trust is to ensure that your partner feels they can trust you with their feelings. The way toward that goal is through empathy, listening, and being open about your own issues.

Fostering Vulnerability in the Long Term

Vulnerability can be encouraged in your partner on a regular basis, and it doesn't necessarily have to be a single thing you need to change at some specific point. How comfortable a couple is with being vulnerable depends on how they carry themselves in their daily life, including subtle changes in behavior and communication. You can partake in certain exercises with your partner to strengthen this bond.

Avoiding the Pitfall of Judgment

As mentioned, judgment is one of the biggest obstacles to vulnerability and openness. While some people struggle with opening up, others struggle to be less judgmental. Just like the fear of weakness, judgment is a problem rooted in some natural human impulses. It has its role to play in other human affairs, but in relationships, what you think doesn't always have to be what you say. Open communication is paramount, but there are different ways to express certain opinions. To become less judgmental, the best thing you can do is learn how to truly listen.

If your partner opens up about something they've done wrong or a weakness they might have, your first thoughts might be negative and critical. You shouldn't be ashamed of these thoughts, but choosing how you're going to externalize your concerns is up to you. One previously mentioned aspect of active listening is especially important when encouraging vulnerability. That aspect is the art of asking open-ended questions. Whenever you see signs that your partner is slowly opening up about something, remember to encourage them by asking questions and formulating them in a way that provides the maximum possible space for them to keep talking.

Apart from employing active listening to encourage your partner to share, you can also choose when and where to address your partner's admissions. Sometimes, the best thing to do is to affirm them when they open up and then schedule a more thorough conversation on the topic later in the day. This will give you time to collect your thoughts and come up with ways to respond with a supportive, non-judgmental attitude.

Self-Reflection and Awareness

While it could be your partner who has a problem with vulnerability, you may also have to have a conversation with yourself. If you find that, time and time again, your partner shuts you out, avoids serious topics, and deflects from their emotions, ask yourself and your partner what you can do to make it easier for them.

Be empathetic and reverse your roles, at least in your mind. Imagine that you're the one who's sharing a deep fear, uncomfortable past experience, or any other troubling concern. Then, list ways you typically respond to your partner's moments of vulnerability, including verbal and non-verbal responses. Do your best to imagine how those responses would make you feel in your own moments of vulnerability. The central question should be whether or not those responses would encourage you to share more or to shut down the conversation. You should also ask your partner for their input regarding whether or not you're a good listener and which of your typical responses make them uncomfortable with sharing. Together, you can create a definitive list of behaviors and statements that make your partner feel judged.

The Importance of Gratitude

Gratitude is an excellent form of encouragement regarding vulnerability, although it's often overlooked. Take a moment to think about a stereotypical group therapy setting, such as support groups for substance abuse. You'll see the perfect example of how gratitude encourages sharing. These groups contribute to creating a non-judgmental space and are usually successful in opening up even the most stubborn participants.

Whenever a participant shares a troubling story, the therapist will explicitly thank them for sharing, and the entire group will validate them. This is easier to do in support groups because they are made up of people with similar experiences, but gratitude as a replacement for judgment is a simple concept that works well in all worldly situations. It could take some training, but you can get the hang of it fairly easily. Whenever your partner opens up about something, make it a habit to respond with something like, "Thanks for telling me," or, "I appreciate you telling me." When this becomes instinctual for you, it will eventually completely replace judgmental statements. How you communicate also affects your mind, so it's likely that it'll evolve past mere speech and gradually make you less judgmental on a fundamental level.

Daily Openness

Being open with your partner should be omnipresent throughout your days together. Vulnerability sometimes entails opening up about something big and very painful, but in most cases, it's found in those little things in life and how you interact daily. The main aspect is to be honest about your feelings regardless of the topic.

For instance, people might avoid admitting that their feelings have been hurt for many reasons. Sometimes, it's their fear of weakness, but there are also cases where people worry so much about their partner's feelings that they completely disregard their own. Telling someone they've hurt you in any way can be just as distressing to the offending party, especially when the offense was unintentional.

If you think about everything you've learned about communication and conflict resolution in this book, you'll remember there are healthy ways to address any concern. Whether your partner has caused you deep emotional pain or simply forgotten to buy the groceries you asked for, the approach is the same. All those minor infractions and annoyances that occur in every relationship are opportunities for you and your partner to practice openness.

Interpersonal Exploration

You should set aside some time weekly to discuss this aspect of your relationship with your partner. A comfortable and controlled setting can be much more conducive to honest expression than a discussion that comes out of the spur of the moment. For instance, discussing your fears with your partner is always beneficial.

Fears are very prone to exaggeration when suppressed and bottled up because your mind has ways of filling certain gaps on its own. Without support and understanding, which includes valuable advice and guidance from the people you trust, your mind will allow the fear to grow – and, eventually, take over. When you externalize it by writing it down on a list or naming different fears with your partner, your fear will likely feel smaller. The insights you get from your partner can also put the fear in perspective and allow you to examine it in a new, more rational light. Whether it's your fears or something else, exploration exercises with your partner will uncover many things you've kept bottled up. You'll often find that the problem only needed a set of fresh eyes, and the solution had been staring you in the face all along.

Section 10: Keeping the Spark Lit in the Long Term

When couples can work together and resolve their problems effectively, these relationships will enjoy a degree of long-term stability – enabling all the nice things in life to flourish.

Suppose you always fight and experience insecurity with your partner. In that case, finding room to enjoy things together will prove difficult. All those activities that happy couples engage in, often naturally and without much thought, are the spice of life that keeps relationships feeling fresh and exciting for a long time.

Keeping the spark in your relationship ongoing is always a work in progress.
https://www.pexels.com/photo/group-of-people-with-sparkling-bengal-lights-4997798/

Some couples need less excitement than others, as many people are perfectly happy spending quiet evenings with their significant other and only occasionally require that need for excitement. If it works, it's certainly not broken, but it's also true that people can sometimes neglect this part of the relationship. These oversights can make relationships less stimulating and fulfilling, producing all sorts of tension. Some people just put up with it and let things run their course, resigned to the idea that losing that spark is normal. It's one of the reasons a very common misconception exists that long-term relationships will inevitably become stale and uninteresting. In reality, rekindling the flame takes just a bit of effort and patience with one another. Nothing more.

The Wonders of Long-Term Partnership

The misconception that long-term relationships eventually lose their spark is all too common and very unfortunate. First and foremost, embracing this mentality can discourage some people from committing to serious relationships or marriage in the first place. However, it also sometimes manifests as an unwillingness to improve relationships in crisis. Some people will end up unhappy in their relationship and resign in apathy, allowing problems to accumulate and worsen because they believe it's just a natural course they can't change.

No matter how long a relationship has been going, there is no reason to accept the apparent loss of vigor and excitement. It's a tragic path because it results in you and your partner missing out on many great things in life. When it comes to marriage, the later years can really be the best time of the relationship if each spouse takes the right steps!

With continuous effort and perhaps some creativity, you and your partner can come up with new ways to keep the fire lit for many years. Effort doesn't necessarily imply hard work, as that's necessary only in relationships in a severe crisis. The effort to keep the spark going for a loving couple comes naturally and is simply made up of all those small but meaningful things you can do to make each other happy on a daily basis. It means activities and ideas you'll both enjoy, fulfilling your lives.

The emotional connection between two people who meet in the world and then decide to spend their lives together is something quite special in human relationships. People are inherently connected to their parents, siblings, and other close family members. As powerful and important as those connections are, they're almost always the default. They're natural, presumed, and often taken for granted. Meeting someone along your journey and making a connection is a whole other ballgame.

It's a sad reality that some people won't have the same luck and will struggle to find someone to truly connect with, or they'll miss out on an opportunity because they fail to put in the effort. The important people you meet along the way have the potential to learn everything about you and understand you in a way that even most parents can't. Having that kind of support in your life is a priceless gift, and that's what makes long-term relationships worth the continuous effort over the years.

Such a support system can unlock a person's potential in ways they never imagined, not just regarding relationships but life overall. Many people walk around with passions, hopes, and dreams that lie dormant or have been suppressed due to a lack of motivation. Many people have had the experience of a sudden ambitious idea or plan for the future, only to rationalize and eventually abandon their ambitions. This is how complacency sets in and makes people averse to change and effort; this kind of lifeless behavior usually happens when you're alone.

When you have someone who truly knows you and has your best interest at heart, they will push back on your inertia and do their best to prevent you from becoming complacent. Whenever you come up with a reason not to pursue your goals, your significant other will be the person to offer a counterargument. They will poke holes in your excuses and remind you of your abilities that you might forget when you're on your own. Living without this support makes it easy to forget its power, but it's worth every effort to hold on to it once you have it.

Long-term healthy partnership also makes it easier to handle failures and defeats in life. Self-deprecation and discouragement will take hold much easier when you don't have someone to remind you to shift your perspective to the bigger image: that one failure is not the end of the world. A loving and true partner will bring out the best in you and constantly remind you of your strengths and virtues, making most failures look like temporary setbacks.

These are only some of how long-term relationships provide stability and serve as a source of motivation. Self-reliance is essential and can get you far in life, but a person can't go through life without stumbling somewhere along the way. That's where a support system with the one who loves you and whom you can trust comes in to make picking up the pieces easier.

Kindling for the Flame

Since maintaining the spark is a long-term endeavor involving a fair amount of creativity, it's a very open-ended goal. What a certain couple will do to keep things going over the years will depend on their individual traits, preferences, and much else. Every couple can and should strive to chart their own path and develop unique activities that they find stimulating. However, it needs to be said that whatever the choice is, compromise from both parties will yield the best results. The kindling that your relationship needs can include anything from hobbies to exciting adventures to how you communicate daily. Still, some ideas can be universally beneficial in most relationships.

Dating Doesn't Have to Stop

Just as you would do to strengthen intimacy, having regular date nights over the years is always a good way to keep a relationship dynamic and fresh. Whatever your age and however long you've been in your relationship or marriage, there is no point where going on dates together becomes outplayed or somehow unbecoming. If you've ever heard someone say something along those lines, you should certainly disregard these stigmas.

Going out to dinner or for a drink, especially in new and exciting places, will break up your boring routine in many ways. It's rarely about the drink or dinner there; it's really about going through something new and exciting with your loved one. It doesn't necessarily have to be the most exciting date in the world, as simply changing the scenery and doing old things in new settings can be enough to mix things up. Dates are open to infinite improvisations and creativity, though, so they can certainly be exciting as well if you and your partner are up for it.

The Power of Spontaneity

You should aim for spontaneity and novelty if things get a bit too familiar. For instance, there is a fine line between a midlife crisis and trying something you simply didn't have the time or money for when you were younger. Suppose there was ever a hobby you or your partner wanted to take up but didn't get around to for any reason. In that case, it might be a stimulating shared activity for the two of you.

Vacations are another great way to spice things up because they, just like hobbies and dates, allow much experimentation and novelty. Surprise vacations and dates can create very fulfilling experiences, but old things can also be tried in new and exciting ways for added variety. For instance, going on a biking trip to a place you used to visit only by car is a very stimulating outdoor activity. Surprises are always guaranteed to create excitement in relationships because intimate partners know each other very well, minimizing the possibility of unpleasant surprises. Plus, it's always nice to be remembered without prompting.

Trips Down Memory Lane

Making experiences out of revisiting dear old memories in your relationship is another activity that can have an incredibly positive effect on couples. This can mean revisiting a place of significance for a vacation, but it can also include various activities that you used to enjoy years ago. Sometimes, people will gradually stop doing the things they enjoy because they simply forget about them over time, distracted by the requirements of life.

Committing to creating memories together and revisiting them is a rejuvenating experience.
https://www.pexels.com/photo/man-and-woman-sitting-on-brown-wooden-table-4554383/

It can be a very rejuvenating experience to relive old moments, passions, places, and activities, especially when combined with spontaneity and surprises. Relational memory in the human mind can be strange in how it associates the things you remember with the things you feel. Taking a trip down memory lane can thus be much more than fun. It can uncover long-forgotten and buried feelings in ways you least expect. An old place or setting that has significance in your relationship's history can trigger a sudden wave of intense emotions that will be just as strong as they were the first time.

Intimacy

Intimacy is something you should continuously work on. Beyond improving your communication and strengthening your bond, it can also keep a relationship exciting. This is because many intimacy-building activities and exercises are stimulating and engaging. You should always try to share your fantasies, hopes, and dreams with your partner, even if they are new ones that didn't occur to you before.

Throughout the years ahead, never forget the importance of all those little moments of intimacy that consistently keep romantic partners close. Whether snuggling up on the couch to watch a movie, just holding hands, or any other kind of basic physical contact, happy couples will continue to do it even in old age. Not everyone expresses their affection in the same way, of course, but you and your partner should create and preserve your own unique language of intimacy and love.

Never Stop Communicating

The ideas for the things you can do to give your relationship the occasional boost are virtually endless. The main thing is to communicate effectively and consistently. Surprises can be great, but partners in a relationship should never be reluctant to voice their ideas for something new that they might be interested in. Conversely, they should not be afraid to voice their concerns or fears either. You can sit down in the evening and formulate a written, multi-year plan for an exciting future with your partner. Envision, in complete honesty, a list of things that both of you would like to do and experience just to bring more fulfillment into your life. Some of these things could be what you would have been unable to do without your partner's support and participation.

Couples who talk to each other with the same openness and willingness through the years are the ones with the best prospects. There is simply no way to deal with the challenges in your relationship if you don't harness the power of communicating with your partner. Without it, you'll never understand what's wrong, what you should do, or what will make both of you happier. When communication breaks down, relationships gradually fall apart or devolve into years of unacknowledged misery. So, remember to cherish trust with your partner and keep it safe from harm.

BRAVING

Every couple has their own story, which means each one will have their unique formula for long-term success in their relationship. Only you and your partner/spouse can do what needs to be done to live your lives in love and understanding for a long time. You should try to take the things you've learned in this book, adapt them, and apply them in the most optimal way to meet the specific requirements of your relationship. That can mean focusing on some areas more than others or crafting a unique toolset that works for you.

That being said, you've also seen that some things are universal in healthy relationships. There have been quite a few interesting strategies developed by psychologists, couple therapists, and other experts over time, which are worth exploring if you and your partner want to try something that's tried and true. Many of these methods go back to the 50 years of extensive work and research conducted by John Gottman and his wife, Dr. Julie Schwartz-Gottman. As mentioned earlier in this book, these methods focus on various aspects of human relationships, but they especially stress the importance of trust.

Brené Brown, a researcher and professor at the University of Houston, developed an interesting concept. She devised it as the acronym BRAVING, simplifying the meaning of trust by breaking it down into seven key qualities and behaviors. BRAVING aims to help people understand things they need to focus on to facilitate long-term trust. You should consider this concept as a method to build trust and sustain it over time. It applies to all manner of relationships, including the one with your partner.

In a way, the BRAVING concept summarizes many of the lessons you've learned in this book, and it's an excellent foundation to return to for reassured and lasting stability in your relationship. It consists of the following elements:

Boundaries – The element of boundaries refers to personal boundaries and personal space, but it also has to do with various other limits. Boundaries are all about moderation, patience, the ability to sometimes say no, and respecting your partner's occasional need to say no. You and your partner must clearly understand what each of you considers acceptable or unacceptable in the relationship. Practicing continuous respect for each other's person, individuality, and personal pursuits is essential to ensuring that your relationship remains a place of comfort and support, as opposed to an overbearing method of control.

Reliability – Reliability is one of the best ways to reinforce and maintain trust. Couples who know they can count on each other to honor agreements and plans will create an environment of consistency and stability. More than anything else, reliability means that you and your partner will consistently follow through on what you say and do over the years. Breaking ten promises in a row and fulfilling one won't offset the damage and make up for letting them down. The key to consistent reliability is understanding one's limits and realizing that keeping promises and ensuring you never overpromise is equally crucial.

Accountability – If you are to resolve conflicts and get to the root of the issues that arise over time, you and your partner both need to acknowledge your mistakes. However, admitting you did something wrong is only the first step. True accountability to your partner means admitting your mistakes while also making an honest effort to make amends and avoid said mistake again. On the flip side, accountability is something that has to be encouraged through patience and forgiveness. If you default to judgment, anger, and stonewalling out of spite, you won't allow your partner to make things right.

Vault – What Brené Brown calls "the vault" is a couple's ability to confide in each other with complete certainty that deeply personal information will remain within the relationship. This goes back to the fact that vulnerability is important in relationships but isn't necessarily a flag you want to fly in front of the whole world. When your partner tells you something sensitive, it should remain between you, as if locked in a vault. Keeping each other's secrets promotes trust and reliability. Consider how you'd perceive someone who constantly spreads gossip or reveals personal information about someone, even if they just met you. You would hardly consider that person trustworthy, and rightfully so.

Integrity – Integrity dramatically affects all your interactions with other people, especially important relationships. It's about doing the right thing even when it's uncomfortable and practicing what you preach. Everyone can declare a set of values they supposedly have, but if they don't embody these behaviors, their value system will hardly inspire respect and admiration. In a way, integrity is about being able to trust yourself and, in turn, building trust with someone else. Taking emotional shortcuts and avoiding necessary discussions just to maintain the illusion of comfort will be detrimental to your relationship in the long run. As Brown explains it, having integrity is putting courage before comfort.

Non-Judgment – Judgment discourages trust and vulnerability and can be the end of relationships faster than you might expect. As you've seen in previous sections, learning to let go of your instinct to judge is essential in relationships because it clears the way for many things that make relationships great, such as understanding, openness, trust, safety, empathy, communication, and much more. You should also not forget the pitfall of self-judgment. If you're too hard on yourself, it can be more difficult to ask for help and open up to your partner. This can cause as much damage as being judgmental toward your partner.

Generosity – In BRAVING, generosity has a lot to do with giving the benefit of the doubt to your partner and how you interpret intent. It's about assuming that they didn't mean to hurt you, to give them the opportunity and encouragement to clear the air and make amends. If they forget your birthday, for instance, the generous thing is to assume that they had a lot going on that day, were busy, or were going through some problems. This opens the way for a constructive conversation instead of getting angry and focusing exclusively on how your partner's failure affects you personally.

Conclusion

As long as you and your partner or spouse love each other and feel that your relationship is worth preserving, there is always hope to solve any problem that comes your way. Remember that all human beings are fallible creatures. Poor decisions will sometimes be made, issues will arise, and life will throw some curveballs your way. It's not uncommon for relationships to start going through turbulence due to the common hardships of life.

Whatever the case in your relationship, the simple truth is that only you and your partner can help yourselves by deciding that you want to fix things. The fact that you've read this book and are looking for solutions demonstrates your commitment to this relationship, which is a great first step. Suppose you do decide that you need professional help. In that case, that's also an entirely valid path to take toward saving your relationship. However, even that will require some engagement with your partner, as you first need to agree to take that step.

The things you've learned in this book should help you in two main ways. First, this information should encourage you to reflect on things and analyze your relationship objectively to identify where the problems reside. Second, you should now know how to address some of those problems.

Once you get a foot in the door and start engaging with your partner the right way, there might be a very positive snowball effect. These efforts will likely be reciprocated when you take steps to get closer to your partner and open up to them. This is especially true if you're engaging with your partner while reading this book, which is the best way to go about it. The more input you seek from your partner, the easier it will get to share ideas and reach compromises.

After all, it's not up to only you to fix your relationship: It's up to both of you to get your entire toolkits together and give it your best shot as a team. At the end of the day, that's what relationships are all about, and if two people can come together to take on the challenges of life itself, then they doubtlessly also have the power to join forces to preserve what they've built.

Part 2: Infidelity Recovery

A Comprehensive Workbook for Healing, Rebuilding Trust, and Restoring Intimacy in Your Relationship

Infidelity Recovery

A Comprehensive Workbook for Healing, Rebuilding Trust, and Restoring Intimacy in Your Relationship

Emma Lancaster

Introduction

Infidelity has ruined plenty of relationships. The devastating havoc it causes leaves many relationships full of potential lying dead in its murderous wake. The people from these relationships are haunted by its ghost, taunted, as they're left to wonder if they could have done something more to salvage the beautiful connection they once shared with this other person. Perhaps you, too, wonder if there's something you can do to save your marriage or relationship rather than abandon ship and mourn your losses. Here's a comforting truth. You and your significant other can save your connection using the right roadmap, sheer determination, optimism, and a desire for love to reign supreme once more.

This workbook is unlike any other on infidelity. Whether you've had your heart broken by your lover's choice to go astray or realize you've made a horrible mistake betraying your faithful partner and want to make things right again, this book is for you. It's full of practical advice, excellent worksheets, and helpful information to help you find the right path out of the maze of confusion caused by infidelity and into the brilliant warmth of a relationship full of unbridled love.

The principles in these pages are clearly outlined, leaving no room for confusion on what to do at each point in your relationship recovery journey. Allow yourself to feel relief knowing you couldn't have chosen a more effective tool to guide you and your beloved back to the joy of connection you once had. If you are both willing to set aside all pride and resistance and work through the exercises in this book together, the question of whether you stand a chance of remaining together in happiness and love will become moot. You'll find your spark once more — and it's not a matter of if, but when. So, are you ready to take back what is rightfully yours? Are you prepared to elevate your relationship beyond the zenith you've witnessed it attain? Then, there's nothing further to be said in this introduction. Begin your journey with the first chapter.

Chapter 1: Understanding Infidelity

Each night, you try to sleep, but you can't. The only thought in your mind is how the person who is lying beside you so peacefully could have made such a grotesque mockery of the trust you placed in them without question. You listen to the steady rhythm of their breath and wonder how they can find peace, especially after they betrayed you so deeply. Every time their phone rings, your heart fills with questions as you wonder what it's about. Is that another person you should be concerned about? Why are they laughing like that? Why does your partner need to leave the room to take the call? Is it someone you know? Someone you've crossed paths with before. Is the way they're looking at their phone something you should be concerned about? Or is your mind so riddled with suspicion and doubt that you're seeing shadows where there are none?

Infidelity can cause you to be concerned about what your partner is doing.

As your fingertips gently trace the lines on your partner's face while they are fast asleep, you wonder how they could have done what they did without a moment's thought about how you might feel. You've committed yourself wholly to this person. Yet, what have you received in return? Betrayal. Heartbreak. Tears and more tears. You wish you could find it in your heart to fully forgive them. You want to give them a chance, but you can't find it in you. One moment, you've convinced yourself that you've forgiven them and let it go. Then, you're analyzing every gesture, expression, and word. The intimacy you once enjoyed with each other feels like a burden now. It's untrue. Tainted. Disgusting.

Everyone says you should forgive and forget. You want to let it go. You know you should. You feel your pain, suspicion, and hurt eating away at your insides like cancer. You want true reconciliation rather than to live with this farce. You want to heal and move past it. There's just one problem. How on earth are you expected to forgive what you can't forget? What should you do about the pangs of agony that rise unbidden unexpectedly? Is your decision to remain with this person and fix things a betrayal of yourself? What does it mean that you've chosen to stick around instead of finding greener pastures or at least being on your own? Are you that desperate? Are you terrified that perhaps no one will see any reason to be with you? Are you secretly afraid that you believe you don't deserve better and that any attempt to leave will prove you right?

These are just some of the countless concerns you have when you have been a victim of infidelity in your relationship. You desperately yearn for answers, but you're discovering there are no easy answers. There isn't a clear path forward. All that's left is the pain you feel from having your heart ripped to shreds by this person that you were so sure would always have your back as you had theirs. You know you love them, but you're also terrified that you may want to hit back. You're afraid you'll never be able to let it go and that this is the beginning of the end. Well, it doesn't have to be like that.

Infidelity and Its Many Faces

Every relationship has boundaries. Infidelity is a flagrant disrespect of those boundaries. It leads to the destruction of the trust that you and your partner have built with each other and shows disregard for the commitment and exclusivity that you share in a relationship with someone else. Infidelity destroys trust, taking only moments to ruin what may have been built over the years, decades, or a lifetime. This description of the core of infidelity may be a little too simplistic because there are so many ways that it plays out. So, to understand what infidelity is, you have to view it in its many forms. You need to peel back the layers, so you know when you are looking straight in the face of this relationship killer.

Physical Infidelity: This form of infidelity is obvious and unquestionable. There are no gray areas when your partner has chosen to be intimate with someone else or you're the one who made that mistake in your relationship. Traditionally, relationships are founded upon the concept of exclusivity, which means there are certain things that are kept between you and your partner. When you commit to one another, there is an agreement that you are the only ones who have access to each other's bodies. You enjoy physical intimacy and sexual interactions with each other and no one else. Physical infidelity can cause deep wounds that are hard to heal.

If you've experienced infidelity in your relationship, you will know all about the feeling of jealousy as you observe your partner interact with others, and you'll feel it even more so if you've attempted to patch things up. You've thought a great deal about how they chose someone else other than you. You feel humiliated because your partner's decision to step outside of your relationship to find sexual fulfillment feels like an indictment on you. It's like they're telling you you're not good enough.

Once upon a time, you assumed you alone had access to their special touch, but now it's clear that's not the case. Each time they touch you, all you can think about is how those same fingers touched another person in the same way. This thought makes you question whether you are special to this person.

Emotional Infidelity: A more subtle form of infidelity, emotional infidelity can be just as hurtful. This form of betrayal is usually slicker and more insidious, so it's not easy for you to pick it up immediately. You can think of it as a slithering serpent, green and blending in with the grass. People who are unfortunate enough to be in relationships with narcissists or other similar personalities will often wonder if they have any right to be upset about this form of infidelity. Their partners gaslight them into thinking nothing is going on because there hasn't been anything physical between them and this other person.

Can you relate to this feeling? If you've ever found yourself wondering at the deep bond your partner shares with someone else, it could be that they are being emotionally unfaithful. The exclusivity in your relationship doesn't just end with sharing your bodies with no one else. Relationships are founded on vulnerability, which means you and your partner share secrets. All your hopes and dreams, fears and doubts, are the things you would never ordinarily share with anyone else. What does emotional infidelity look like? It could be sharing your worries and concerns about your relationship with someone outside of that relationship. This person isn't a regular friend, and what you're sharing isn't even something you've mentioned to your friends. On the surface, it appears as if there's nothing going on, but really, what's happening is you have begun to prioritize this person, and there is a shift in where you channel your intimacy. You begin relying on this person emotionally more than you do your partner.

Emotional intimacy could also look like flirtation. For instance, your partner may spend countless hours chatting with an acquaintance that they find interesting. You notice there's lots of laughter between them at first blush, which doesn't appear to be a problem. However, the laughter is a result of many inside jokes that your partner doesn't share with you. On top of that, these people often communicate with inappropriate double entendres. While your partner may want to insist there's nothing serious going on there, you feel you have been relegated to the sidelines in your relationship. You and your partner used to be lead actors in your relationship. Now, you've been demoted to the role of an extra.

Cyber Infidelity: Since the birth of social media, cheaters have been more creative than ever. They have countless avenues to be unfaithful to their partners. The sad capitalistic world you're in is one that actively endorses this behavior. Don't you think so? Check out the Ashley Madison scandal if you're not already familiar with it. This is a company set up with its entire business model centered on enabling people to cheat on their partners, and while it may sound like a dystopian movie plot, it is the reality of the world today. Cyber infidelity covers everything from flirtatious texting to entire affairs online. You'd think the inability to connect with a person physically should deter the possibility of infidelity. Well, think again. The Internet is a playground full of opportunities for illicit connections, riddled with traps to ruin even the happiest of marriages and relationships.

Cyber infidelity is another insidious form of unfaithfulness. What makes it even worse is that it's tough to confirm this without having to snoop or pry into your partner's business — unless divine providence intervenes and you happen to see something by accident. The paranoia from discovering cyber infidelity is so intense that even after resolving things or moving on to a different partner, you can't help but worry every time you see them on their phone or laptop. An everyday activity that is unavoidable in today's world becomes a trigger. It takes time and effort to trust that this person isn't up to no good after you've experienced this form of betrayal.

Regardless of the form intimacy takes on, it still hurts. Even if you used to be a trusting person, that trust is now utterly destroyed. At best, you decide not to suspect your partner, but your mind remains permanently open to accepting the chance that there may be something going on that shouldn't be. Infidelity leaves you confused about what could have gone so terribly wrong between you and the person you love that they had to be unfaithful. You find it hard to release your anger over their decision to hurt you in this way. Your pain and frustration blind you to the fact that sometimes, people are imperfect and make mistakes. That sentence wasn't meant to shift the blame to you or force you to forgive. You don't owe anyone forgiveness. You owe it to yourself so you can finally move on and live a full, happy life after infidelity.

Why Did They Do It?

Infidelity doesn't happen out of the blue. Certain factors create the perfect cocktail of emotions and thoughts that lead to cheating. Here's a look at some of the issues that built up to this catastrophe.

Communication Problems: At the heart of most problems in relationships is communication, or a lack thereof. Before the incident that rocked your world happened, were you and your partner struggling to communicate with each other? Did you find that countless times, rather than speak up, you'd say, "Never mind"? Is there a remarkable difference between how you and your partner communicated at the beginning of your relationship versus now? Does it feel that so many things are left unspoken or swept under the proverbial rug? When there's too much dirt beneath the rug, it's only a matter of time before one or both of you decide to look away from it completely, to pretend it's not there. When things get this bad in a relationship, some people turn to work while others will be drawn to the next shiny person. It's not every time that an unfaithful person is looking to cheat. They may want someone they can share their problems with. They want someone who understands them. If your partner could find the words, they'd tell you they were seeking connection, and that's why it happened.

A lack of communication can cause infidelity.
https://www.pexels.com/photo/man-wearing-brown-suit-jacket-mocking-on-white-telephone-1587014/

Needs Unmet and Desires Unfulfilled: When you're in a relationship with someone, you both have expectations of each other. There are certain needs that can only be fulfilled by the other person. You and your partner need emotional intimacy. Your relationship thrives when you stimulate each other intellectually. It's even better when you have passions in common because they offer you more opportunities to strengthen your bond. If you've gone too long with those needs unmet, what do you think is likely to happen? Not only is that the perfect breeding ground for resentment, but if you give in to the temptation, you'll get your needs met elsewhere. Sometimes, unfaithfulness comes from needing to fill the hunger for these desires. The unfaithful partner forgets they can communicate their need to their partner. Instead, they look outside the confines of the relationship, which is now a desert and are drawn in by the mirage of an oasis of fulfillment in the arms of another.

The Decline and Destruction of Intimacy: When intimacy in a relationship disappears, there's a storm brewing, and the fallout will be catastrophic. Why? Relationships can't survive without intimacy. Some people erroneously assume that intimacy is only about physical touch. However, there's far more to it than that. Surprisingly, it's possible for you and your partner to engage in sexual relations regularly and yet still feel disconnected from each other. How so? Realize intimacy also involves emotional vulnerability. It's about the many things you share that make you laugh and cry. When you're intimate with your partner, you both have secrets that you share freely.

However, if the intimacy between you erodes over time, you'll feel neglected. You and your partner never resolve any conflicts because it appears there's no point anymore. After all, it's not as if the resolution will lead to a reestablishment of intimacy. So why bother? This line of thinking causes one or both partners to seek a connection with someone else. It's like you're both stuck in the middle of an emotional tundra, and you're desperate for any source of warmth, even if it's only the flame of a match. You forget that if you both set aside your egos, you can create a roaring inferno of warmth and intimacy once more.

Pressures from Without, Problems from Within: If Disney had their way, life would always be happy. Everything would always be peachy. However, real life has a habit of throwing you curveballs. Sometimes, those curve balls come with so much force that they devastate everything, including your relationship. It could be a financial problem, the loss of a job, or having to take on a new job in a different location. It could be a health problem or some disagreement in the extended family that's starting to affect your relationship. Whatever the case, these external factors leave an indelible mark, and when you and your partner don't work together to mitigate the effects of these problems, it leads to a fire at home. What happens when one of you isn't present during these tough times? Being human, they'll desire comfort and solace. So, it's not a stretch to see how they may escape into someone else's arms to ride out the overwhelming storm. While handling storms by creating more storms is not a logical or effective strategy, it's the reality of life and relationships.

The Thrill of the New: Some people are unaware and unprepared for the monotony and boredom that will occasionally happen in a relationship. They expect constant thrills and excitement. So, when the initial spark dies down, they get bored. It's natural to settle down into a routine in a relationship, but for this type of person, routine feels like they're stuck in a rut. They want to break free because they feel like their life is slowly being drained out of them. These people find it inconceivable that you can remain with one person for the rest of your life. So, they deliberately engage in infidelity because they need some element of unpredictability to keep things exciting. To them, there couldn't be anything as interesting as cheating and hurting the person they claim to love. If you're the partner who's been cheated on, and this is the reason the other person gave, it can hurt like nothing else. They gave up the stability and promise of forever with you for something fleeting.

Your Emotional Journey after Infidelity

When you experience infidelity, it causes a deep wound that makes you feel unbearable pain. You may as well have been physically battered and bruised because you feel raw at the betrayal. You find yourself reeling from emotion to emotion because it's difficult to get a grip on yourself in this state of mind. When the unexpected happens, you react in the most unexpected of ways. However, here's a breakdown of what you may experience as you become aware of the betrayal.

You're in a State of Extreme Shock and Denial. The first time you discover your partner has been unfaithful, it feels as if you've had the ground pulled from beneath you. Your brain isn't entirely sure how to process this information. It was never something that entered your mind, even when you had rough times with each other. So, you find it beyond belief that this person who claims they are in love with you could do what they did. The shock is so severe that you choose to be in denial instead. If you can deny the truth strongly enough, perhaps it'll prove to be a lie. Of course, there's nothing logical about denial, and yet it's understandable because you desperately hope that this is not real. You're grasping at straws, hoping to find anything to prove this is only a cruel joke or perhaps an unrealistic nightmare.

Your Denial Gives Way to a Tidal Wave of Emotions. When you finally realize that this is real, you feel so many things at the same time. You feel grief because the relationship you thought you had with this person is gone. You're overwhelmed with anger because you can't believe this person would take advantage of your trust and love like this. Your sense of betrayal runs so deep that it causes bile to rise in your throat, burning bitter like acid. You think about your partner with the other person, and you are immediately overcome with jealousy about what they have done with each other and whether your partner made love to them in the same way they did with you.

Denial gives way to a tidal wave of emotions that includes grief.
https://unsplash.com/photos/grayscale-photo-of-woman-right-hand-on-glass-nwWUBsW6ud4?utm_content=creditShareLink&utm_medium=referral&utm_source=unsplash

When you realize you're being jealous, you feel self-loathing. You're supposed to be mad at this person rather than feeling jealous. Your mind recalls every seemingly innocent interaction you've seen your partner have with this person, and it feels like a knife being twisted into a fresh wound, going deeper and deeper with each turn. You wonder if you were so insecure you refused to see the truth under your nose because you didn't want to lose your partner. Then you wonder if you are somehow responsible for their actions or if you're the problem because you are "not enough."

You're Overwhelmed by the Long Road Ahead to Re-Establishing Your Relationship. Your trust is gone now, and the only way to replace it is through a lot of patience and time. Your partner has expressed remorse over their actions and wants to fix things. You'd like to do the same but have no idea how to be vulnerable again. You feel like a detective when you begin regaining what you lost. You analyze every conversation and scrutinize every weird inflection in how they speak. You realize forgiveness is not something that happens instantly. It's a decision you must make each day until it finally takes root in your heart and blossoms.

Every narrative around infidelity is unique. It comes down to the individuals and the relationship with their different personalities and the dynamics of their connection. There is also the real effect of culture on the problem of infidelity. Some people have wired their minds to be ready and willing to forgive infidelity because they've accepted that people are imperfect and make mistakes. For these fortunate people, they don't have too much trouble getting over the hump. However, not everyone is so lucky. If you don't know how to navigate life after infidelity, you're not alone. It is possible, though. You can rekindle the spark once more.

The way you view infidelity depends on your attachment style, which was created in your early childhood days. If you are an anxiously attached person, you are always afraid of abandonment. So, if you've experienced infidelity, it feels like a confirmation of your fear. On the flip side, you may have trouble expressing yourself emotionally if you have an avoidant attachment style. Desperate to protect your heart, you shut down, making it hard to engage in the reconciliation process.

The Ripple Effects of Infidelity

When the stone of infidelity has been tossed into the pond of your relationship, it sends ripples that continue to travel past the spot where it sank. Here's a quick look at some of those devastating effects.

How the Betrayed Partner Is Affected:
1. They have to deal with the feelings of shock and anger. After getting over these initial reactions, the grief and pain from the betrayal are intense. The emotional laws can get so bad that they're

riddled with anxiety and depression, and their self-esteem takes a critical hit.

2. Infidelity leaves a long-lasting psychological impact on the betrayed partner, inflicting PTSD. If you were the one betrayed, you become hyper-vigilant. You're constantly looking over your shoulder and terrified of becoming intimate with anyone. You may also experience flashbacks and have trouble trusting people or taking them at their word.

3. It's not only your future relationships or romantic prospects that are jeopardized. If you've been betrayed, you'll also lose trust in the people you call friends and family. You isolate yourself because the way you see it, if someone you were in love with could do what they did to you, who's to say that others aren't as deceptive? So, you isolate yourself.

4. Overcome by the emotional anguish, you may find it difficult to perform and be productive at work, which could jeopardize your prospects.

How the Unfaithful Person Is Affected:

1. If you cheated on your partner, you feel guilt and shame. You're unable to look at yourself in the mirror. Your guilty conscience leaves you riddled with anxiety. You judge yourself for making a terrible decision, and, as a result, you lose your sense of self-worth.

2. When your partner reassures you, they trust you, but you find it hard to believe. Your sense of guilt makes it nearly impossible to relax and accept intimacy in your relationship.

3. By choosing to be unfaithful, you ruin your reputation. Your family and friends may decide to distance themselves from you, and if this information makes it to your professional life, there may be repercussions.

Seeking Professional Help

There's nothing as devastating as being in the middle of infidelity. The typical response to it is to isolate yourself from the people who could offer you support during this difficult time. You would be doing yourself a huge favor by moving in the opposite direction. Even better, you should seek the help of a professional to embark on your healing journey. A professional can offer you helpful coping mechanisms rooted in actual psychology that will help you move past your pain and mental blocks toward reconciliation.

You and your partner could go for couple therapy. Why should you bother with this? Couples therapy is the perfect setup to allow you to communicate openly and honestly about your feelings with each other. The therapist will be present to mediate the conversation and ensure everyone is heard. Also, couples therapy provides you with a neutral space so everyone can focus on the root issues that caused the problem. If you decide to take this route, you and your partner have to be willing to put in the work. Recognize this is not a magic pill that will solve everything in one session. There needs to be hard work, and the process is challenging. Both of you have to draw on your reserves of resilience to pull through this dark time.

If you don't care for couples counseling, you could always go for individual therapy – a great option if your partner is uninterested in working with a professional. You have a safe space in which to be honest and process what you feel. If you're already doing couples therapy, you could tack on individual therapy as well because it'll offer the opportunity to address your problems. For instance, you may want help working out feelings of guilt, insecurity, and self-esteem problems, issues that may have led to the infidelity or worsened it.

Finally, support groups are also an excellent option. If you go this route, it's essential to choose one with an experienced facilitator who is qualified to handle infidelity. You'll love support groups because you will realize you're not the only one with your problem, and you can draw strength from others there with you.

Before wrapping up this chapter, you should know there's no right way to react to infidelity. You're a human being, and this is a complex phenomenon. So, never beat yourself up for not handling things the way you think you should have. If you were the unfaithful partner and you deeply regret your actions, you have to stop feeling sorry for yourself and channel that energy toward rebuilding the bond between you and this wonderful person who loved and trusted you. The only way to make it through this storm is by being empathetic with each other and making self-reflection a daily practice.

Chapter 2: Processing Emotions and Healing Wounds

What happens after infidelity? It would be so much easier to handle if it was a regular wound. You clean it up, bandage it, and call it a day, waiting for it to heal quickly. However, the same can't be said for infidelity. The mess it leaves behind is horrible and will require much work to sort through. You can't afford to leave your emotions the way they are. You can't suppress them because they'll come up in all kinds of ways and make it impossible to reconcile with your partner or find love in the future. You have to address them, and that's not an easy thing to do.

Many emotions can come out after experiencing infidelity.

Emotional Responses to Infidelity

The betrayed person and the betrayer will experience a myriad of feelings that can be confusing. Sometimes, they're downright contradictory. If there is to be any hope of successfully processing your emotions, you must first know what you're likely to feel in the aftermath of a relationship breakdown.

You'll Feel Furious with Yourself and Your Partner. When you think about the injustice of the situation, it makes you mad. You made vows to each other, yet your significant other had no problem breaking them. You're furious at this third party who has come between you and snatched the once-sacred intimacy. You're furious at yourself for ever daring to trust someone else with your life. Merely looking at your partner's face sends you into a tailspin of rage. What was once the face of your lover becomes the face of a snake, a deceiver who had no trouble hurting you. Your fury fuels your sense of judgment as you say you'd never do the same thing they did. Your rage may be driven by a sense of righteous indignation.

You're Overcome with a Sense of Betrayal. You were supposed to be a team, and now you aren't. Your relationship was built on a solid foundation, and now it has been utterly ruined and shattered into little pieces. All the blood, sweat, and tears you put toward maintaining a loving connection with this person have been for nothing. The memories you created as a team are now nothing more than sources of pain and anguish, highlighting the absurdity of the situation you're in and causing you to question everything, and no answer will ever be good enough.

Your Heart Fills with Sadness. The sadness comes from an awareness that the dreams you once shared are now gone. You're mourning the loss of your relationship because even if you managed to fix things, it will never be the same. You're sad because you long for the days when you could confidently say your partner would never do what they just did to you. You miss your innocence and naivete. Your partner may be right next to you, but because of their actions, it feels as if you're all alone. For the first time in a long time, you feel abandoned and have no idea what to do with yourself.

You also Feel Afraid. Your partner's actions have raised a lot of insecurities and fear in you. Does their unfaithfulness mean you are unlovable? If you forgive them and move past this, does the fact that they've done it once mean they could do it again? When they go to work, are they really going to work, or are they taking a detour to somewhere they shouldn't be? When your partner says it's daylight, should you trust their word? Sure, the sun's shining, but can you trust your eyes? After all, you trusted them once before, and look where that got you. Your mind becomes paranoid.

You Feel a Sense of Shame. Whether or not it's true, you assume people think you are the reason for this mishap. After all, why would your partner cheat on you if you weren't the cause? You start to buy into that narrative. You find yourself mulling over what you could have done to deserve being betrayed this way. The shame causes you to punish yourself. You're also ashamed that you didn't see it happening before you found out. You're not psychic, but that doesn't keep you from punishing yourself with shame anyway.

The unfaithful person isn't exempt from emotions either. Here's a quick run-through of what they'll experience.

1. They feel guilty as they remember every moment of their deception and unfaithfulness.

2. Overcome by the sudden clarity of getting caught, they feel confused about what drove them to be unfaithful in the first place.

3. They're also afraid because they have no idea what the consequences of their actions will be. They recognize there's a chance they'll lose the person they love the most and other relationships when their deception is discovered.

4. They're sad about all the times they've broken promises and lied and how deeply they've wounded their partner.

5. They're ashamed of themselves, well aware that they allowed their lesser selves to get the better of them. They can't see themselves as anything more than a destroyer of dreams, and they're humiliated by realizing what they've become.

Identifying Triggers

You could be merrily going about your business when you're suddenly hit with intense feelings over what happened because something has flung you far and hard from the present into the past. It's like you're smack in the middle of the worst of times. When this occurs, it's because you've been triggered emotionally. What is a trigger? Anything that makes you suddenly feel an intense wave of emotions reminding you of something traumatizing you've been through in your past. When you understand the many emotional triggers that could cause strong feelings, you can do something to prepare for them. You could be triggered by anything from a song you and your partner used to love to a special place where you used to have dinner or even specific behaviors you may see on television or elsewhere that your partner used to do. Triggers can hit you any place, any time, so you must be prepared.

If you hope to process your emotions effectively, the first thing you must do is identify the things that trigger you into feeling overwhelmed by them. If you don't take the time to identify the things that cause you to feel the negative wave of emotions, you leave yourself susceptible to a breakdown at any time. So, how do you identify what's triggered you? Whenever you become overwhelmed by negative emotions, you need to mentally retrace your steps and notice what you were doing or thinking right before you started drowning. Once you have identified a trigger, you should write it down in a journal to keep track of it. The following is a list of possible triggers you may have to deal with.

1. Beware of special days like anniversaries, holidays, birthdays, and other days you and your partner may have celebrated regularly.

2. You may be triggered by certain movies or songs that remind you of your partner or the affair.

3. If there are places you visited together when things were better, you may find them triggering now.

4. Did you walk in on your partner being unfaithful to you? Then trust that that area is now an emotional landmine. There's no way you won't be triggered each time you're near that space.

5. If you smell something that reminds you of your partner, that could be a trigger.

6. Specific items of clothing and jewelry could also trigger an emotional reaction.

7. Any mention of the person your partner cheated on you with is a definite trigger.

8. Social media posts that refer to your partner or the person they cheated on you with could trigger you into feeling upset. It's even worse when you see pictures or videos of them together.

9. Are there any gifts or keepsakes from your relationship? Holding on to them could trigger you into an explosive emotional reaction.

10. You may feel triggered if something in your partner's body language or tone indicates they may be deceiving you.

Sometimes, when you're triggered, it's not because of something happening outside of you. For instance, you may have intrusive thoughts that remind you of what you and your partner went through. It's not unheard of to have nightmares about this unfortunate event whenever its anniversary rolls around. You may assume you've put it behind you, but your mind hasn't. This is why it's vital to process your emotions healthily rather than attempt to suppress them.

Underlying Emotional Issues

You want to move past the problem. You'd like to get on with your life already. Yet, for some reason, you can't. What gives? It could be that you have underlying emotional issues from way back in your past that make it difficult to process your emotions after infidelity. Here's a look at some of these stumbling blocks.

You May Have Experienced a Traumatic Childhood. If you were neglected as a child or abused in any way, these are experiences that never go away. Your body grows, and your mind knows more things now than when you were young. Still, the scars remain. Nothing has changed. A traumatic childhood makes it difficult to trust people or build intimate connections with others because, in your mind, you've drawn a parallel between relationships and pain. The people you should have been able to trust as a child failed you repeatedly. They may even have abandoned and neglected you. They didn't need to use actual words to tell you that you are not worth anything to them. Their actions said at all, and you internalized the messaging. You now think of yourself as insignificant and unworthy of love. So, when the incident happened, it only reinforced what you already unconsciously thought about yourself.

Past Betrayals Can also be a Barrier to Processing Emotions. If you've experienced betrayal in any form or been deceived, it leaves you with a mark you can't wipe off. You view every interaction with the people in your life through the lens of suspicion. Since your partner betrayed you, you feel even more justified in suspecting their every move. Also, being the victim of repeat betrayals makes you feel more insecure and distrustful. These things make it nearly impossible for you to heal.

You're Dealing with Grief. You could be grieving a parent or some other relative. If you've lost a relationship that was important to you, it can put you in a fragile state of mind, making it impossible to process the pain of infidelity, let alone the confusing maelstrom of other emotions that come with it.

Your Attachment Style Is Getting in the Way. If you have an anxious attachment style, you need to be constantly reassured by your partner that they're there for you. Their engagement in infidelity is anything but reassuring, and it triggers your fear of being abandoned. Your response is to be more controlling and clingier, refusing to let your partner out of your sight. This won't do you any favors. Are you an avoidant? As someone with an avoidant attachment style, you work hard on building walls and shutting everyone out. Even a tiny little bug can find a small crevice to let it past your fences and domes! Any attempts to salvage the relationship will be countered by your desire to remain independent.

There is also the disorganized attachment style. People with this style have trouble remaining in relationships for the long haul. If you are someone who relates to this, your caregivers were not consistent in the love they gave you, as they offered you security only to take it away. You have come to expect the same inconsistency in your relationship and don't do anything to fix it.

Low Self-Esteem Makes Things Difficult. Rather than be objective and constructive in how you handle the emotions from the aftermath of infidelity, you find yourself wallowing in shame and blame. If this is your struggle, you cannot squarely put the responsibility for the relationship's breakdown where it belongs. You forget there are two people in a relationship and instead shoulder all the blame yourself. It sounds like this only affects you, but the truth is, you'll resent your partner for reminding you of how you feel about yourself deep down. So, if the two of you are to have any hope of fixing things, you have to address your self-esteem issues.

Low self-esteem can be an effect of infidelity.

These are just a few of the many underlying factors that could exacerbate the emotional damage of infidelity. The question becomes, how do you move past these challenges? It all begins with self-reflection. By making a daily practice of introspection, you'll become aware of your triggers and the other emotional issues that have remained dormant and unaddressed for years.

Tools and Strategies for Self-Exploration and Processing Emotions

Mindfulness: Mindfulness is about bringing your awareness to the present moment. By staying present, it is easier to become more self-aware and catch the thoughts and feelings that well up within you to analyze, understand, and release them. Find a quiet spot where you will not be disturbed or distracted for at least 15 minutes, and ensure you are dressed comfortably in loose clothing. You may sit on the floor or a chair or lie on your back.

Close your eyes and bring your attention to your breath. Your mind will wander to other thoughts besides your breath, and that's fine. As soon as you notice you've been distracted, all you have to do is return your attention to breathing. The purpose of this exercise is not to remain undistracted but to continue returning your mind to the present as often as it takes. You'll get the best results if you make this practice daily.

Journaling: Journaling is an excellent way to become aware of your inner world. You should have a dedicated notebook for this exercise and do it daily. The magic is in the consistency. Write about your feelings for the next 10 to 15 minutes. Don't attempt to censor yourself in any way. You can use the following questions to guide your journaling:

- "What do I feel right now?"
- "What do I think about my partner betraying me like this?"
- "What am I most afraid of?"
- "What other occurrences from my past remind me of this?"
- "What is it I need the most right now?"

Once you've finished journaling, review what you've written. Compare it to your previous entries and see if you can pick up on any recurring themes. Doing this will make you more aware of your emotions, and it'll be easier to process and let them go over time.

Mindfulness meditation and journaling are excellent tools to help you become more self-aware. Not only that, but you can also use them to deal with intense feelings of resentment and anger. If you want the best results, consider journaling straight after your mindfulness meditation.

Healthy Coping Mechanisms

If you want to process your emotions effectively, you must also take care of yourself. In other words, you must find healthy and constructive ways to release the intense feelings. Are you feeling overwhelmed? Pick something from this list and see how it helps you.

Exercise can release the pent-up anger.

1. Work out, dance, or move your body in some way that releases the pent-up anger and boosts your feel-good hormones.

2. Express yourself through art, writing, singing, or any other creative medium you love.

3. Go out and become one with nature. Rather than sit at home ruminating, go to the park, beach, forest trail, or anywhere else full of Mother Nature's gifts. You'll feel grounded after a few minutes in the great outdoors.

4. Eat healthy, and you'll do wonders for your body, which is connected to your mind. You'll think better and have more resilience to handle triggers when they occur.

5. Get good sleep. Never negotiate how long you should rest for each night. Seven to 8 hours is a good target to help you feel refreshed.

6. Be with the people who love you. Even if you're feeling raw and hurt, their presence will ground you and remind you that there's still some good left in the world. That reminder will help you bounce back whenever you feel affected by a tsunami of emotions.

7. If it all gets too much, you should seek professional help from a qualified therapist who can help you find your way through the fog and see the light again.

Emotional Check-in Guide for Couples

Whenever you and your partner struggle emotionally, you should use this emotional check-in guide to help you rebuild your connection and find firm footing with each other. Wherever you choose to do this exercise, you should not be interrupted. Setting the mood is helpful, so make it somewhere cozy and comfortable. Trying to do this exercise in glaring light could work, but adjusting the scene to encourage intimacy is far better. Also, before agreeing to this exercise, you both must ensure you have the time and that no pressing matter requires your attention. All your devices must be turned off. Remember that this period is specifically for you, your partner, and your relationship. Any notification on your phone can wait until later. Kick things off by sharing what you appreciate about your partner and let them do the same. Whatever you do, never start this exercise without gratitude. You need to positively prime each other to be receptive, open, and vulnerable, and there's no better way than clearly stating how you appreciate the other person. After this, ask each other these questions:

1. "What specific emotion are you feeling right now?"
2. "What would you like to share about how things have been for you emotionally lately?"
3. "What's the one thing I could offer you that you need the most from me right now?"
4. "How do you think I've been feeling recently?"
5. "From everything I've shared with you so far, what are the things you resonate with?"
6. "In what ways do you think we could be more supportive of each other in dealing with our emotions?"

You must be fully engaged in this exercise. Keep your eyes on each other and affirm each person's response with your body language, whether through a nod or a well-timed touch. Always remain supportive and validate the other person when they tell you how they feel, even if you feel guilty or disagree. Remind yourself that the goal of this exercise isn't to fix the other person. If you do that, you're telling them they're broken, and that's disempowering. Instead, channel your focus toward understanding how they feel and where they're coming from. Are you the sort of person who likes to offer solutions? You would be better off keeping that tendency in check and simply offering your partner a listening, supportive ear. When you've finished asking each other these essential questions, you should wrap up the same way you started: by appreciating each other.

Emotion Identification Exercise

You can't manage emotions you don't know, can you? Here's how to identify your emotions.

1. Check in with how you're feeling. If you feel several emotions, write them all down. When you've done that, put them in three groups: Positive, Neutral, and Negative. Positive emotions include gratitude, happiness, joy, ecstasy, etc. *Negative emotions* are obvious. They include anger, hate, fear, anxiety, resentment, etc. *Neutral emotions* are those of contentment, boredom, or curiosity. Write it all down in your journal.

2. Is there an emotion you're shocked to have discovered you feel? Write it down. If there is more than one, get it all out onto your journal's pages.

3. Turn your attention to your body. What unique sensations can you pick up on? Do you feel butterflies in your belly? Is your face feeling flushed? Is your chest tight, making your breaths shallow? Write down how the emotions you feel show up in your body.

4. Finally, it's time for self-reflection. Ask yourself these questions:

    a. What do you think triggered your emotions?

    b. What patterns have you noticed, if any?

    c. What could you do right now to feel better right away?

Feelings **Worksheet**

Name	Date

Think of **a prominent feeling** that you're experiencing and want to explore:

On a scale from 1 (not feeling at all) to 1 O (most intense), **how intensely** you're feeling this right now:

Why are you feeling this way? Describe your thoughts

How does your body respond to this feeling?

How does this feeling affect your behavior?

How does this feeling affect others?

How often do you feel this way?

Do you think this is a positive or negative feeling?

If you want to change this feeling, what are some ways you can overcome it?

Chapter 3: Being Open and Honest

Do you want your relationship to thrive? In that case, you must be willing to be open with your partner. Both of you must communicate honestly with each other, and that can be difficult to do sometimes. Why? Sometimes, it's obvious that your partner cannot hear certain things without feeling hurt. However, both of you need to recognize this and set aside pride to listen to what the other person is saying. If you don't commit to this before you attempt to communicate, somebody will wind up feeling hurt, which will only compound your problems. Since you are dedicated to restoring your relationship, you must be willing to practice transparency. You have to communicate authentically and keep your dialogue respectful in the process. If one person feels like they can't communicate from a place of truth, this will only be a recipe for more resentment.

Being honest can help you begin solving your problems.
https://www.pexels.com/photo/colorful-honest-text-4116566/

Why Openness and Honesty Matter

Openness and Honesty Are the Only Ways to Build Your Trust. Anything else shatters the confidence you have in each other. If you want this back, you have to be transparent with each other. There's no room for guesswork. You both have to cover all your bases so no one has to guess your motives. You have to be transparent with each other at all times about how you feel. In this way, your relationship stands a chance of working out.

When You're Both Vulnerable, You Can Be More Empathetic to Each Other. It is impossible to be vulnerable when you don't communicate. Sometimes, what your partner says will be difficult to hear. However, you need to be present and actively listen to them. They owe you the same as well. You both have the right to talk about how you're hurt, what you need, and what you're afraid of without feeling like you're going to be judged. By being open and honest, you remind each other that, at the end of the day, you're both humans. You build a bridge that allows you to reconnect with each other once more.

Communicating Honestly Can Accelerate the Healing Process. If either of you feels they can't be honest about their emotions, resentment will build up. Resentment makes the wound more infected. So, choose honesty instead. When you're both honest, you can diagnose the root cause of the problem. You acknowledge the pain you've caused each other, and this is how you can process the trauma that you're experiencing and heal from it.

Openness Fosters Growth. Without self-reflection, there's no way to communicate authentically about your feelings and thoughts. Self-reflection is a process that always leads to personal growth and development. So, in a roundabout way, being open and honest in your communication will encourage you both to become better people. Therefore, you'll improve your relationship by leaps and bounds.

So now you're convinced of the necessity to be open and honest with your partner. How can you encourage each other to be authentic and vulnerable? Whatever time and space you fix for this conversation has to be conducive to the rawness of open, honest interactions. In other words, you both have to agree this is a safe space without judgment or criticism. You can be raw and honest about your feelings, thoughts, and experiences without being put down or made to feel invalid. Transparency is a two-way street in your relationship, so no one should be doing the emotional heavy lifting here. You're in this together. It's up to both of you whether the ship sinks or remains afloat. So even if you are not the person who stepped outside the relationship or marriage and betrayed it, you also owe it to your partner to let them share their thoughts and feelings.

Barriers to Open Communication

You should be aware of the obstacles you will likely face when you attempt to communicate openly with your partner. In this way, you have effective strategies to head off those problems before they can further sink their teeth into your relationship. The following is a list of the barriers you will face and how to handle them.

1. **The Fear of Judgment:** When this comes up, reassure your partner using words and nonverbal communication. Try holding each other 's hands or comforting each other with a hug as you speak. Whenever you talk about how you feel, only use I statements so you don't leave your partner feeling worse.

2. **The Fear of Conflict:** Sometimes, people refrain from speaking honestly because they expect arguments and fights. How do you get over this fear? Both of you need to be on the same page and look at your conflict as a chance to grow and understand each other better. Adopt a "you-and-me versus the problem" mindset rather than a "you versus me" frame. Remember, you're working together to restore your relationship. So, you have to be on the same team.

3. **Past Grievances and Hurts:** Be willing and quick to acknowledge how you've hurt your partner. Don't make any attempt to sweep your wrongdoings under the rug. You may feel upset because they're bringing up something you thought was already resolved. However, don't dismiss them by telling them it was a long time ago. Instead, gently talk about what happened. Acknowledge your part and apologize again if needed. When you do this, you can remove those past issues from the present and not worry about them clouding the current conversation.

4. **Emotional Outbursts:** Sometimes, things may get heated between you as you share your honest opinions and feelings. The best strategy is to schedule a timeout. It would be a good idea to have a safe word – something neutral that you can say to each other

whenever you feel you're about to lose control of your emotions. This way, before you can say or do something damaging as a result of your wild emotions, you step back from the conversation and cool off.

5. **Low or No Trust:** Unfortunately, this problem has no immediate fix. You can rebuild trust by consistently being honest and following through on your promises. This will require time and patience from both of you.

6. **Different Styles of Communication:** If you're the kind of person who prefers a direct approach, you should let your partner know. The same applies to your partner. Have you noticed that either or both of you prefer a softer way of communicating difficult truths? Then go easy on each other.

These strategies are excellent for when difficult questions or brutal truths have to be shared. If you remember nothing else from this section of the book, there is one thing you should always keep in mind that will ensure you remain honest and open with your partner. The secret is the willingness to be vulnerable with each other. Rather than allow your pride, anger, or pain to cause you to build up walls, you should do the courageous thing and tear down the obstacles between the two of you. Vulnerability is about sharing aspects of yourself that the other person may not like but trusting that they will still love and accept you as you are. You know that what you share can be used to hurt you. Yet, you set your pride and ego aside for the sake of your love.

Here's a story of Layla and Kevin: Months after Kevin had betrayed Layla by having an affair, there was clearly some resentment between them. Things eventually hit a breaking point, and the two clashed. Layla was frustrated because Kevin refused to tell her everything, leaving her to use her imagination. Also, Kevin wasn't telling her he was ashamed of himself, and that's why he wasn't speaking about it. Layla would eventually find the courage to be vulnerable. She told Kevin she wanted to know everything because it tore her apart not knowing. She told him she would make peace with his answers even if they hurt. She helped him understand they could finally find freedom and peace by sharing the truth.

Kevin dared to reciprocate Layla's vulnerability by answering every question she asked. It wasn't easy to sit there and listen to him. She ran the entire gamut of emotions, from disbelief to anger, shock, and pain. However, she finally understood. By the end of that conversation, Kevin and Layla looked at each other with new eyes. After many months of pain, anguish, and resentment, it became evident to them that their love was still there and could be nurtured back to full health. However, they'd never have known this if they hadn't been willing to finally be vulnerable.

The "I" Statement Exercise

You and your partner need to pick one instance from the past where you communicated terribly with each other because of the unfaithfulness that has rocked your relationship. Then, follow these instructions:

1. Each of you needs to reconstruct the argument in writing. This time, however, you will state your points using "I" statements. In other words, rather than saying, "You made me so mad when..." or using language that indicates you're attacking or blaming your partner, rephrase by writing, "I felt so mad when..."

2. Have the same conversation again, but use your revised statements this time. Ensure you sound assertive yet calm.

3. If you have anything further to add to the conversation, remember to keep using "I" statements.

Discussion Time: Take Turns Answering These Questions

1. Did you find these "I" statements made it easier to express your feelings?

2. What changes did you notice in the tone of the problematic conversation from before versus now?

3. How do you think these "I" statements can help when you're communicating with each other in the future?

Role-Playing Conflict Resolution Exercise

You'll need a timer and two chairs placed opposite each other.

1. Pick a specific situation that often causes arguments or conflicts in your relationship. It may or may not have anything to do with infidelity.

2. One of you has to act as yourself, while the other acts as a neutral third party observing them. Set your timer for two minutes.

3. Play out the problematic scene, but use "I" statements as you speak honestly this time. The point of this exercise is not for you to win a debate or a prize. It's to practice how to effectively communicate your thoughts without causing harm to the other person.

4. If you're playing the part of the neutral observer, you have to pay active attention. Rephrase what the other person is saying in your words to ensure that you are clear on their meaning. Is there a point that has you confused? Ask questions until you gain clarity on their driving emotions and motivations. No interruptions, please, and you can't make judgments either.

5. If things devolve and become too heated, you can take time off from this exercise and try again in a few minutes.

6. When the timer goes off, switch roles.

7. At the end of this exercise, you both need to discuss how participating felt. What was it like observing from a neutral standpoint? What was it like sharing your opinions using "I" statements? Compare notes with each other. See what new things you have learned; what communication patterns in your partner have you now seen? Brainstorm to come up with different ways that you could approach conflict in the future.

You and your partner can restore the trust and love that you once had for each other. In fact, it's there, but you just need to discover it, but there's no way to tell if you don't do the work. You have to commit to being open and transparent with each other. You also have to make peace with the fact that sometimes transparency means you will get hurt. In those times, remind yourself that the only way to grow individually and as a couple in a relationship is to use the feedback to develop the union you desire. You must be patient with each other because your trust will not be rebuilt in a day or even a week.

Before wrapping up this chapter, one more thing must be said: If you're the guilty party, refrain from being frustrated with your partner because they cannot always let go of the pain. Even if you assume that your infidelity happened a long time ago, you have to remember that for your partner, the discovery is fresh. So, give them the grace of patience and time.

Chapter 4: The Healing Path to Forgiveness

After infidelity, you and your partner need to heal individually and heal your relationship together. It is impossible to heal and move forward if there is no forgiveness. Forgiveness isn't only a matter of the wronged person forgiving the offender who stepped out of the relationship or marriage. It's also about forgiving yourself, whether you're the perpetrator or the betrayed. As the person who was cheated on, you may not think you need to forgive yourself, but you have to do some self-reflection to be sure you're not blaming yourself for what happened. Unfortunately, it's not uncommon for people who have been cheated on to take on blame and shame. If you continue journaling and mindfulness meditation, you will discover if you hold any anger or resentment toward yourself for what happened.

Forgiveness can help you heal.

On the flip side, if you're the one who trashed the vows of your marriage, you will feel terrible about yourself. You clearly have your work cut out for you, as you need to acknowledge your human imperfection and forgive yourself before you and your partner can move past this. If either person in your relationship has trouble setting themselves free from self-blame, it will be tough to heal and move on. Unforgiveness, whether of your partner or yourself, will always rear its ugly head, reminding you of the painful incident and refusing to let you out of its grip. Therefore, there's no escaping the work of forgiveness if you both want to return things to how they were, or even better, between you.

What Is Forgiveness?

Imagine you're at the base of Mount Everest. You're wearing nothing but a sleeveless top and beach shorts. Your feet are clad in flip-flops. You have no food, no water, and no equipment. You have one task: to climb the mountain before you, as you are. If you don't, there will be terrible consequences. That's how difficult it is to forgive after infidelity. Fortunately, unlike the scenario you've just imagined, it's not impossible. So, what does it mean exactly? Forgiveness isn't about forgetting. Asking people to forget the wrongs they've experienced at the hands of others is unfair and impossible. There isn't a magic delete button in your brain that can get rid of specific memories. Also, certain things will trigger the memory of what happened. Does the fact that you remember those things occasionally mean that you haven't forgiven your partner? Absolutely not. This fact has to be stated right now so you don't erroneously assume you haven't forgiven this person because you can't forget what happened.

If forgiveness isn't forgetting, what is it? It's a deliberate, conscious, continuous choice to release the anger and resentment you feel against yourself or your partner. The key word is continuous. Forgiveness is a skill. How do you master a skill? Every skill in life can only be mastered through consistent practice. Some people would have you believe forgiveness happens all at once. If you accept this logic, you'll find yourself frustrated. It is a gradual thing. If you commit to the process one day at a time, you'll discover you no longer hold any grudges against your partner or yourself. You'll know you've accomplished it when you finally feel at peace.

The Psychological and Emotional Dimensions of Forgiveness

Developed by Professor of Psychology C. Raymond Knee and Kristen N. Petty of the Department of Psychology, Oregon State University, Corvallis, implicit theories of relationships are key discoveries in the psychology of relationships. They are a critical part of how forgiveness works in the context of infidelity. There are two ways you could look at your relationships.

1. Destiny beliefs
2. Growth beliefs

If you have destiny beliefs about relationships, you believe that things are meant to be -or *aren't*. It's similar to having a fixed mindset but in the context of a relationship. You don't think you or your partner can change. You assume that every relationship has its set of problems, and while that is true, you also think that things like infidelity are a clear sign that you and your lover are fundamentally incompatible. In other words, you don't believe the problems can be fixed. In that case, you are less inclined to try to forgive or patch things up. The more realistic choice for you would be to move on with your life. Even if you choose to remain with your partner, you're not holding your breath, expecting them to be faithful. They could be sincere about never wanting to commit the same offense again, but somewhere in the back of your mind, you're waiting for the other shoe to drop once more.

If you have growth beliefs about relationships, you know that relationships need work. Except there's no such thing as a perfect relationship. That's no excuse not to develop what you have with your partner. Your growth beliefs indicate that whatever challenges come up, they are simply opportunities to develop more intimacy and connection. So, even in the face of a challenge as difficult and painful as infidelity, you are constantly looking for ways to leverage that problem and turn it into something good for both of you. Research indicates that you and your partner have a higher chance of forgiving each other for your mistakes — including infidelity — if you have growth beliefs.

Other psychological dimensions of forgiveness include:

1. **The Quality of Your Relationship Before Infidelity Happened.** If you and your partner enjoyed a strong bond and were happy with

each other, there's a higher chance you'll pull through this.

2. **The Threat Level:** If you are the aggrieved person and you feel your relationship is terribly at risk on account of the infidelity, it will be harder for you to forgive.

3. **The Degree of Blame:** If the person is sincere and proactive in accepting blame and demonstrating remorse, there is a higher chance that you will forgive them. The person who cheated must take responsibility, not just in words but through actions.

Worksheet: Identifying Your Relationship Beliefs

Part 1: Self-Reflection

Instructions: You and your partner need to do this exercise individually. First, read the following statements, then pause to consider them thoughtfully. When you're certain of your true sentiments, rate how much you agree with each statement on a scale of one to five, with one being "strongly disagree" and five being "strongly agree."

1. I believe that this relationship was destined to happen.
2. I believe this relationship could become better with time and effort.
3. I believe having to put in effort to make a relationship work is a clear sign it's not supposed to be.
4. I believe that every relationship needs work and has to be nurtured for it to be successful.
5. I believe every problem or challenge I encounter in this relationship is a clear sign it should end.
6. I believe all the problems I experience in my relationship with my partner offer a chance to grow and improve together.

Scores: Statements 1, 3, and 5 are destiny belief statements, while statements 2, 4, and 6 are growth belief statements. Look at the score separately for each set of statements. The higher of both results will show you whether you have destiny beliefs or growth beliefs.

Part 2: Discussion

Instructions: Once you and your partner have finished with the first part of this worksheet, it's time to discuss the answers you have to the following questions:

1. Do you have growth beliefs or destiny beliefs?
2. What were the statements you strongly disagreed or agreed with, and why?
3. How have you noticed your beliefs about relationships affect how you react to the problems you face?
4. In what ways might your beliefs affect your ability to forgive unfaithfulness?
5. Are you willing to change some of your beliefs or work on them? If so, what beliefs do you want to adopt instead?

Remember that the goal of this worksheet is to help you and your partner understand each other and communicate clearly. No one is right or wrong for having different beliefs from the other person. Also, it's fine to change what you believe with time rather than right away. The point is for you and your partner to work together on your relationship and strengthen it.

The Benefits and Transformative Power of Forgiveness

While there are many reasons to forgive each other in a relationship, infidelity is one of the toughest problems to navigate. It is a cardinal sin; forgiving it can feel like moving a mountain with your hands. Fortunately, facts trump feelings, which means even though forgiving is impossible, you can do it. You should want to forgive because there are many benefits to letting go. If you think this process is about letting the other person off the hook, there's more to it than that. Forgiveness is about dropping your burden so you can breathe easy and live a blessed and fulfilling life.

Do you want to have happiness and peace of mind once again? Then, you need to forgive your partner for their infidelity. If you refuse to let this go, it will also taint your relationships with other people. Forgiveness is about demonstrating to yourself that no matter how badly someone has treated you, you can pick yourself back up. From this powerful position, you have no trouble relating and connecting with other people in your life because you know even when they slip up, you can trust yourself not to hit rock bottom and stay there. So do this for the sake of all the other connections that you value. Forgive yourself for this, if for no other reason. Know that anytime you're offered the opportunity to forgive someone of a transgression, you have the chance to grow in resilience and strength.

The following is a list of benefits of forgiving infidelity:

1. **You and Your Partner Have the Chance to Grow Together.** By choosing to forgive your significant other, you offer each other a clean slate from which you can rebuild the relationship. You discover the depth of the love you share.

2. **You Regain Your Trust.** While this isn't an automatic process by deciding to forgive your partner, you are saying that you'd like to reestablish a connection and work toward trusting this person again. If your partner is sincerely sorry about how they've wronged you, they will take this olive branch and work hard to show you they can be trusted.

3. **You'll Get Closure.** Holding a grudge in your heart for so long without closure does no good. Forgiveness offers you the opportunity to release the guilt, shame, and hurt so you can turn your attention to creating a beautiful future that isn't saddled with the weight of past mistakes.

4. **Forgiveness Is Wonderful for Your Mental Health.** Whenever you hold a grudge against someone, even if it feels righteous and justified, you only poison yourself spiritually and mentally. By choosing to let go, you drop all the stress of feeling like you've been wronged. You pump the brakes on the negative thoughts that nag you daily as a result of this injustice you've experienced. Compare negative thoughts to positive ones; you'll find the former is a burden to bear and the only ones that ever weigh you down.

5. **You Can Develop Better Intimacy.** When you forgive, it's saying to your partner that you want to start over. It's releasing all the terrible emotions that keep you from connecting. Forgiving automatically makes you want to better understand each other's feelings and thoughts. As a result of the mutual understanding you've developed, it's only natural that you become more intimate with each other. The bond between you will grow even stronger, so you never have to worry about repetition. You have to admit it would be so much easier to be with someone who you are certain would no longer hurt you that way than to have to start afresh with someone else who you are uncertain of because you need time to get to know them.

It should be immediately apparent to you how these benefits of forgiveness transform your relationship for the better. Think of the best times that you had with your partner before the infidelity occurred and realize that things can be even better than that now — only if you are willing to be courageous and take the steps required to let go of the past. Having said that, it is pointless if the person in the wrong is not prepared to do what it takes to fix your relationship. If you find yourself in this situation, you should still be willing to forgive them regardless of their lack of remorse but prepared to completely let go of the relationship, as your sense of self-worth must be guarded at all costs.

Worksheet: Grasping the Importance of Forgiveness

Write your answers in a journal to make the most of this worksheet. This way, you can reflect on them later.

Part 1: Appreciating the Effects of Forgiveness

1. Think about how you've been doing emotionally. In what ways do you think your ability to forgive could help you feel better than you do? How do you think your emotional and mental health may be boosted by choosing to let go of the hurt and resentment in your heart?

2. What is the current state of your relationship? How can forgiveness help you and your partner develop a deeper connection?

Part 2: Are You Ready to Let Go?

1. Take some time to reflect on how you feel about the infidelity. On a scale of one to 10, how prepared are you to forgive this person you promised forever to? Make a list of all the things you think stand in the way of letting go of their mistake; then, reflect on how you can overcome those hindrances.

2. Set some time aside to speak candidly with your partner. Let them know about the concerns and fears you have that make it hard for you to be willing to forgive them. As you discuss with them, weigh up how remorseful they are and what they've done so far to show you they want to fix things. After your conversation, journal how you feel about whether or not you sense they are genuinely prepared to rebuild the trust they destroyed.

3. Check-in with trusted family and friends. Sometimes, the pain you feel may make it impossible to see through the confusion from this sudden change in your relationship. If that's the case, you should be willing to seek guidance from your people. Your therapist will also have valuable input to offer you. Once you've checked in with them, consider the insights you've gained from your conversations with them and journal about how they may help or hinder your ability to forgive.

Repentance, Forgiveness, and Reconciliation

Repentance, forgiveness, and reconciliation are all inextricably linked. It is far easier to forgive when someone who has done something wrong is obviously very sorry about it and willing to do all they can to repair the damage they've caused. In other words, repentance is a show of remorse because the wrong party truly understands the impact of their actions on you. They seek to repair, mend, and bind the wounds in the hope that they can heal. When you're in a situation where your partner isn't remorseful about what they've done, it's easy to feel resentment toward them. However, in this case, forgiveness is the better option, not for them, but for you. In such situations, your decision to forgive them isn't because you intend to let them do the same thing again or get away with it but because you care for yourself. By choosing forgiveness, you set yourself free to move on from the hurt and pain and prioritize your joy.

While forgiveness happens on the inside, reconciliation is on the outside. It is a two-person job in the context of your marriage. You and your partner work hard to build the trust desecrated by infidelity. The reconciliation process means you can't afford to keep secrets from each other anymore. You have to be open and honest with each other, as you've already learned. Neither of you can afford to hold back on your concerns and fears, so you have to be vulnerable.

Reconciliation requires a painful conversation about the truth behind why what happened. It means each of you has to be willing to be held accountable for your part in the deterioration of the relationship. The best premise to have this conversation on is one where you're both open to listening to each other, even if you don't quite agree. Being defensive does not help the reconciliation process because you invalidate your partner when you argue their points. The reconciliation process focuses on brainstorming solutions to help your relationship become more resilient and impervious to infidelity or any other problematic storm that could happen to rock it.

It is possible to forgive without reconciling. However, if there is to be reconciliation between you, there must be forgiveness. If you're both on the same page about wanting to pick up the pieces and start afresh, then remorse is not optional. Remorse isn't about using flowery words to talk about how sorry you feel and how you'll never do the same thing again. It is about putting your money where your mouth is and taking action to show your partner how truly sorry you are and how desperately you'd like to repair your connection.

Worksheet: Stages of Forgiveness

There are various models with different stages of forgiveness. Forgiveness is a very individual process that depends on who's forgiving, their life experiences, the factors surrounding their marriage or relationship, etc. However, no matter the forgiveness model, certain themes pop up repeatedly because experts have identified them as the most crucial stages to true forgiveness and release. When you're ready, go through this worksheet. Take as much time as you need, and take breaks in between if you find you're emotionally overwhelmed, okay?

Stage 1: Acknowledge the Hurt

1. Do you recognize you've been badly betrayed and hurt? Don't be quick to answer this one, even if the answer is obviously a resounding yes. When you've reflected and written your answer down, think carefully about the various ways you may be attempting to suppress your pain or downplay what has happened, whether in your thoughts, words, or actions. Write it all down.

2. Describe in detail what happened. Get a factual play-by-play of the infidelity on paper, and don't be afraid to be specific and clear. This will help you acknowledge the extent of the damage.

3. Next, acknowledge your hurt. You have to look at how this affair has affected you. What are the effects on your emotional well-being? Do you feel lost, paranoid, or betrayed? What about your physical health? Are you having trouble sleeping or eating? How has this affected your connections with others? Write every way you've noticed the infidelity has affected you.

Stage 2: Consider Everything

1. Journal about the state of your relationship before the affair. This is meant to help you see circumstances that may have pushed your partner to it. Avoid wasting your energy playing the blame game or judging your partner because the goal is to understand what may have driven them unfaithful. Replay things from their perspective, too.

Stage 3: Accept Reality

1. Realize that the infidelity did happen, and there's nothing that could change that fact. Write about how it's best to accept the truth of what occurred.

2. This step requires setting your journal aside and allowing yourself to feel the full brunt of your emotions. Let these emotions flood your mind and body. Why? You can't release them otherwise. They're ugly, but fully experiencing them is necessary in order to forgive. You can set a timer for ten minutes before going on to the next step.

3. Realize you alone are responsible for your feelings. Yes, this sounds harsh because your partner's actions triggered these difficult emotions in the first place. What happens now, though? You alone can decide to heal.

4. In your journal, commit to accepting that you cannot control the past or your partner's choices in the future, but you can control how you respond to this event. This is where you figure out whether you want to forgive them, fix things, or forgive them and move on with your life. Either way, you must release your propensity to hold on to the past and commit to moving forward. Don't assume you're no longer supposed to feel hurt or betrayed from this point on; instead, you're deciding to take back your power from this event in the past and dictate how your life will proceed from this point on.

Stage 4: Determine What's Next

1. This is a visualization exercise. Picture your life five or ten years from now. Pretend to be a fly on the wall, watching you and your partner interact in an everyday scene. Then, imagine your partner leaving the room, and you materialize before your future self. What does your future self have to say about your decision to stay with your partner?

2. Here's another visualization exercise. You're five or ten years in the future this time, and you're not with this person. What is your future self up to? How do they seem? Materialize in front of them after observing what their life is like. What does this version of your future self have to tell you about your decision to let your partner go?

3. Journal your experiences in both visualizations and then take some time to consider your next course of action, understanding that regardless of your choice, you should forgive them for your own sake.

Stage 5: Repair the Relationship

1. As the hurt person, if you choose to forgive, you have to draw up an action plan for the process. First, journal about how you can encourage open communication between both of you.

2. There's no fixing things without getting clear on your boundaries. So, what are the boundaries you can set for yourself to maintain your sanity and emotional well-being through the repair process? Also, what are the boundaries you want to set for your partner to help fix things, and how can you communicate them clearly and respectfully? Make a plan to determine your partner's boundaries for you, if any.

3. Ask yourself what your partner could do to help in the trust-building process. Consider ways you can help as well.

Stage 6: Learn from the Experience

1. Talk with your partner to see what they've learned about the experience. Journal about it, and share your insights on the whole issue up to this point.

2. From the insights you've gleaned, what ways do you think you could prevent this problem from rearing its ugly head in the future? Have your partner brainstorm ideas, too, and share your plans with each other.

Stage 7: Forgive

1. This is when you commit to forgiving your partner, remembering it won't happen in a day, nor does it mean you'll never remember it. It's simply a decision that each time resentment, anger, sadness, or betrayal wells up within you, you'll seize that as an opportunity to release more of the darkness and heaviness until you're lighter.

Worksheet: Reconciliation

Use your journal, as always. These exercises are for both partners but should be done individually first before you share your answers.

Part 1: Why Do You Want Reconciliation?

1. What are all the reasons you'd like to reconcile with your partner? Go into as much detail as you can in your journal.

2. What would you like to experience as a result of initiating and sticking with the reconciliation process?

3. Are there any possible stumbling blocks you're worried about tripping over as you try to mend things with your partner? Write about them in detail.

Part 2: How Do You Talk to Each Other as You Reconcile?

1. Draw up a plan of action about how you'll share how you feel with your partner and what you expect by choosing to be vulnerable with them.

2. Now, with your plan in hand, could you come up with some ideas to keep the communication between you and your significant other flowing honestly and openly as you reconcile? Write it all down.

3. When you and your partner inevitably butt heads with each other or don't see eye to eye, what's your plan for how to handle those difficult times with as much love as possible and to keep the fallout minimal at worst or nonexistent at best?

Part 3: How Do You Forgive Yourself and Your Partner?

1. Write in detail about forgiveness as you see it, both for your partner's actions and your own.

2. Now, what actionable steps could you take to encourage the energy of forgiveness to flow freely in your relationship?

3. When you're in the middle of a resentful or angry moment, how do you handle it? Could you draw up a list of things you could do to keep your focus on your desire to forgive and reconcile? Do that right now, and refer to this plan when the bitterness hits you out of left field.

Part 4: How Do You Rebuild Your Trust?

1. What should your partner do to restore your trust in them and the relationship? If you're the one who broke the trust, what things do

you think you could do to mend your partner's confidence in you?

2. In your opinion, what are the best milestones to track how well you're both doing in building trust and loyalty?

3. This isn't an easy one, but it's necessary. What do you intend to do if trust is broken once more during the reconciliation process?

Part 5: What Happens After?

1. When you and your partner finally reconcile, how do you see your relationship compared to this rough, uncertain period?

2. Are there specific changes you strongly desire to see once you've moved past the problem of infidelity?

3. Now, you need to write a commitment to your partner about how you'll deal with any similar situations or temptations that could lead to another break of trust in the future.

4. Finally, if you were the one who was betrayed, write a commitment to yourself about what you'll do the next time you find your trust has been broken. If you're the one who broke the other's trust, write a commitment to yourself about how you'll handle any situation like this in the future and nip it in the bud rather than hurt them again.

When you've finished, you can share your worksheets and discuss anything that stands out to you as worth exploring further.

Worksheet: Building Empathy

Step 1: Create an Environment That Feels Safe for Both of You. This should be quiet, without disturbance, distractions, or devices. A safe space also means not feeling the pressure of other obligations like work, so you're both in a serene state of mind and can focus on being in the here and now. So, you'll both have to agree on a time and place and commit to being there for each other to make this exercise successful.

Step 2: Talk about All Your Feelings, One after Another. You'll need to take turns and can't afford to be less than honest. However, don't assume being honest gives you carte blanche to disrespect the feelings of the other human before you. So, as you share how you feel, ensure you're using "I" statements, owning your emotions and responses rather than placing them on your partner's shoulders — regardless of whether they cheated on you or not.

Step 3: Listen to Each Other Actively as You Share Your Concerns, Feelings, and More. Your attention should be on what your partner's telling you and not the goal or working out what to say in response. Your goal is to understand them, and that means you shouldn't interrupt or let your mind drift. Your partner will feel safer sharing if you indicate you're listening through brief sounds of affirmation, nodding, or other body language.

Step 4: Reflect on What You've Learned and Offer Sincere Validation. Reflect on what they've shared with you because this shows your partner you're listening and makes them feel validated and safe. For instance, you could tell them, "What I'm hearing is you feel deeply betrayed and hurt, and the pain you feel is beyond describable."

Stage 5: Demonstrate Empathy. When you put yourself in their shoes and see through their eyes, it's not hard to empathize with how your partner feels. Do this, and then say something to show them you understand why they feel how they feel. Acknowledge your part in triggering these difficult emotions within them.

Step 6: Now, It's the Other Person's Turn. Repeat steps one through five. When you've done that, you could wrap up with a hug and thank each other for taking part in this exercise despite how difficult it is.

Chapter 5: More Trust-Building Tools

After infidelity, the process of building back the trust you and your partner once had is arduous and takes a fair bit of time. You have to be willing to commit yourself repeatedly before you can see results. This chapter seeks to help you with the best tools, advice, and exercises to help you pull your relationship back from the precipice and possibly take it to even greater heights than you both thought possible. First, you should know what trust is really about.

Trust is the foundation of any relationship.

What Is Trust?

No relationship can exist without trust, and expecting a relationship to do so is like expecting a body to live without a heart or life to continue without water. Trust is the sole reason intimacy is possible. Without it, you can't feel secure in your relationship, and you'll have trouble understanding each other. When there's trust, there's vulnerability, which feeds the closeness you have with each other. This willingness to be vulnerable is why getting betrayed hurts so badly because the idea behind trusting and being trusted is you can both share the bits of yourself that no one else gets to see. So, to know that all that safety has been threatened by infidelity makes it tough to trust again. Trust, in a nutshell, is the willingness to strip off all the masks and costumes you've put up to get along with everyone in society and to lay yourself bare, warts and all, for someone else to see and accept you as you are without judgment or criticism.

Frequently Asked Questions about Trust

Q: "Can I ever trust again once I've experienced infidelity?"

Yes, it's absolutely possible. You may feel like your inability to forget what went down means your ability to trust is shattered, but that's not the case at all. You can rebuild the trust between yourself and your partner, and by putting what happened in the correct perspective, you'll find you don't have trouble trusting. If anything, you'll be inspired to take a critical look at your connections with friends, family, and colleagues and see how you can encourage more openness and honesty by demonstrating your willingness to hear people out, even when the truth is ugly.

Q: "Is it possible to trust my partner, considering they've cheated on me?"

You have the ability to trust them. Sure, it will require your partner to show you they're also well aware of what they've done wrong and putting in the effort to reassure you that their mistake is a one-off. It will also require bravery on your part by being willing to meet them halfway, giving them the benefit of the doubt. You'll both need to be more open than you've ever been with each other, but you can swing it.

Q: "How long will it take me to build back my trust once I commit to the process?"

The process will take as long as it takes since every couple who struggles with the effects of infidelity is different. Generally speaking, the process could take months or even years, depending on how eager you are to mend things.

Q: "If the person I love truly loves me, why did they break my trust in the first place?"

Many factors contribute to people making poor choices like cheating, which affect their relationship or marriage for worse for a long time. However, you should know it's not your fault that your partner cheated. It would be unfair to take responsibility for damage you didn't cause.

Q: "Is it a cause for concern that I'm struggling with trust after my partner's unfaithfulness?"

No. It's perfectly normal and a natural response to being betrayed. If someone's making you feel like the bad person for not being able to trust your partner right away, they're wrong. *You don't need that sort of toxicity in your life.*

Self-protection after betrayal is a natural protective mechanism. When ancient humans tried new plants and fruit as they foraged, they would find out that not everything that looked edible should be eaten. Therefore, they were more careful and did all they could not to eat things they'd confirmed were poisonous. Whenever they came upon similar plants or fruit resembling the ones that seemed poisonous, what did you think they did? They were *cautious* because they remembered what had happened previous times. However, they didn't lose their trust; humans would have rather limited food options than no options at all! The point is that it's natural to be mistrustful, cautious, and hesitant to let your guard down when someone has hurt you. You're justified in feeling this way — but realize it doesn't have to last forever and shouldn't because that would be poisonous to your well-being.

Q: "Why do I feel so ashamed and foolish for wanting to rebuild the trust between myself and my partner since they had no trouble doing what they did?"

You may be considering what others may think or feel about your decision. While your friends and family will offer advice from a place of love and concern, at the end of the day, you're the one who decides whether or not to pull the plug on your relationship. If anyone judges you for choosing to repair and rebuild, that's their problem. They aren't you, so there's no way they'll know the nitty gritty about your relationship with your partner. You don't have to feel ashamed, and you shouldn't think of yourself as a fool. You don't have to explain your decision to anyone if you don't want to.

Q: "Will I be able to salvage trust after this?"

You can, and if you both can be honest and open while working hard at it, you will. Once more, it's a long process, but the good thing about processes is they will bring you to an expected end as long as the two of you work on this like it's a project and you're a team.

Now you have the answers to some of the most frequently asked questions regarding infidelity and rebuilding trust, it's time to get to work on repairing the damage.

Trust-Building Tools for the Unfaithful Partner

Tool #1: Complete Transparency. If you want to show your partner you can be trusted, you must be transparent about everything. If you've been transparent in the past, your goal is to go above and beyond everything you've ever done to stay open and clear about your thoughts, intentions, whereabouts, choices, etc. You may assume that transparency is about talking about the things you did during your infidelity, but there's so much more to it than that. You must be willing to share everything about the other parts of your life — and not just what's happening now, but any plans you may have made without telling your partner. If there is such a thing as ruthless transparency, that's what you should be doing. There's no such thing as too much information after you've been unfaithful to your partner and are looking to regain their trust.

Tool #2: Consistent Behavior. Inspiring trust in your partner is impossible if you are inconsistent in your behavior. What does that mean exactly? Consistent behavior means you disclose everything about your plans and actions. If your partner asks you questions, you don't hold anything back because you feel uncomfortable. It is their right to know the answer. So, you have to answer truthfully. Your words must be backed by your actions. Otherwise, you give your partner more reason to doubt you. So, consistent behavior is about constantly showing your partner that you are committed to rebuilding trust through your actions and words. The more predictable you are, the more reliable your partner will find you.

Tool #3: Ownership of Mistakes. When you own up to your mistakes, you must have a face-to-face conversation with your partner. Obviously, you should be prepared before you tell your partner you'd like to talk to them. You must have deeply reflected on what you did wrong and how badly it hurt your partner. When you speak to them, admit your mistakes and help them understand what drove you to breach the trust you once shared. While explaining your actions and taking ownership of your mistakes, you should avoid making another mistake: being defensive or blaming things or people outside of yourself. The whole point of this tool is recognizing that you are responsible and letting your partner know that you are taking accountability for your misdeeds. If you get defensive or make excuses for your actions, you only antagonize and hurt your partner even more. Owning your mistakes is also about being committed to change. So, tell your partner how you intend to improve things, and if you care about them, follow through.

Tool #4: Actions. Flowery words mean nothing if you don't act on them. Also, taking one step does not atone for what you did wrong. Remember, you have to be consistent in your behavior. So, if you want to rebuild trust with your partner, ask yourself what positive things you can do that will demonstrate to them you truly are sorry and want to change. Do you need to manage your time better? Was the infidelity caused by a lack of bonding time between you and your partner? In that case, it would make sense for you to develop a plan of action to help you with better time management. Did you have trouble understanding your partner or communicating with them? Was this why you felt driven into someone else's arms? Do what you can to encourage openness and honesty each time you connect with your partner. If you have to take a class on relationship communication, you should do that. The point is you should show your partner that you are remorseful so your partner can see you're not all talk and no action.

Tool #5: Individual Counseling. It's possible that the things that led you to being unfaithful to your partner are problems unique to you. Whether you're sure of this or not, you'll benefit from seeing a therapist for individual counseling. If you genuinely want to ensure you never repeat this, you need to understand the real reasons you breached your relationship's trust, and there's no better way to figure out the nuts and bolts in your head than by seeing a counselor. You may be surprised to discover deeper layers of insecurity and fear that motivated you to act in a hurtful way to your partner. The good news is once you learn about these things, you can work on them to become a better person. By gaining the light of self-awareness through individual counseling, you're less likely to make the same mistake in the future.

Individual therapy can help with self-awareness.
https://www.pexels.com/photo/person-in-black-pants-and-black-shoes-sitting-on-brown-wooden-chair-4101143/

Trust-Building Tools for the Betrayed Partner

Tool #1: Communicating and Expressing Your True Feelings Openly and Honestly. When you have been hurt, you need to be open about how you feel, not just for your sake but for the sake of the relationship. By expressing your feelings to the other person, they'll understand the extent of the damage they've caused with their behavior and are more likely to be spurred on to do more to fix things. If you attempt to suppress how you feel by telling them it's okay and trying to let them off the hook easily, you do yourself a great disservice. You need to stand up for yourself, and that means sharing how your partner's betrayal has made you feel. This doesn't mean you have to be disrespectful, rude, or vengeful in how you tell your partner. Remember, the best way to communicate if you intend to rebuild this relationship's trust is by using "I" statements to claim ownership of your feelings.

    Tool #2: Setting Personal Boundaries. As a person who has been betrayed in a relationship, you need certain things in place to make you feel safe. Setting boundaries is an effective way to restore the feeling of safety in your relationship that your partner's infidelity has destroyed. Your partner may do their best to help you feel safe and trust them again. However, they are not a mind reader and may be unable to tell when they engage in certain behaviors or speech that leave you insecure and full of questions. What's better than sitting and stewing over every little thing they do? You have to set boundaries.

Let your partner know when they're doing something you find unacceptable and will no longer tolerate. Help them understand what your needs are and what you expect from them so they know not to deviate. It's much better to tell your partner your boundaries than expect them to know them. Why? When you let them know what is and isn't okay, and they still go out of their way to disregard those boundaries, you'll know for certain that you need to end things with this person who disrespects you. Your boundaries should be in line with your values. Do things like respect, love, understanding, communication, and honesty matter to you? Your boundaries should be centered on those values. It's also fine if you discover new limits to rebuild trust in your relationship. Simply communicate them to your partner as you find out about them.

Tool #3: Attend Couples Counseling. The candid truth is that you can only do so much to repair your relationship by using workbooks and watching videos. All of these tools are supplementary at best. It would be much better for you to consult a professional counselor specializing in relationship and marriage matters. You see, your relationship is unique. It is different from every other one out there. Therefore, there's only so much cookie-cutter advice can do for you. That's not to say that using this book will not work. However, to give yourself the best shot, you should see a couples' counselor to address specific issues relevant to you and your partner. Dealing with the specifics is a great way to mitigate the chances of experiencing infidelity in the future and forge a stronger, unbreakable bond between you and your significant other.

Tool #4: Setting Joint Goals. Remember, your relationship is a joint project. You cannot rebuild trust in isolation. You're a team, so you must work hard to restore your relationship to its former glory and possibly even improve it. When you come together to figure out your goals for your relationship, there is a greater chance that you'll succeed at rediscovering your love and trust for each other. You're more willing to cooperate because it doesn't feel like one person is doing the emotional heavy lifting for everyone else. Some goals you can work on include personal growth, better communication, more quality time with each other, better transparency, more patience, etc.

Worksheet: Active Transparency

Write your answers in your journal and reflect on them when you're done.

Part 1: What Does Transparency Mean to You?

1. In painstaking detail, describe what transparency means to you.

2. Consider why transparency matters to your partner, yourself, and your relationship. Write them in detail.

3. Think about the times when you haven't been above board with your partner, which has caused you and your partner to struggle with intimacy or understanding. Write about those events and how you could have handled them better by being transparent.

Part 2: Reflect on Your Past Choices.

1. Write down everything you've done in the past that your partner has no clue about. This isn't the time to censor yourself or hide anything, not if you want to return to a place of trust and peace in your relationship.

2. When you've got it all down on paper, ask yourself why you never told your partner these things, and write down your answers.

3. Finally, you will disclose all of this to your partner in a letter, ensuring you clarify that while your goal isn't to hurt them but to be above board with them, you understand that the fact you've withheld things will hurt them. Let them know you want to move forward with rebuilding your trust if they're open to it, and that's why you want to throw all your skeletons out of the closet and onto the floor.

Part 3: Get to Work on the Trust between You.

1. What do you think could make it difficult to be truly transparent with your significant other, and how would you deal with them? Write it all down.

2. Draw up a plan for regularly letting your partner know where you are whenever you're not together.

3. Write about how you think your relationship could benefit from your decision to be more transparent about where you are, who

you're with, what you're up to, how you're feeling, and everything else your partner should know.

Part 4: Getting Feedback and Adjusting as Needed.

1. It's time to share your plans to be more transparent with your partner. The goal is to find out what they think about it and look for ways you can make it work together.

Worksheet: Creating a Relationship Vision Board

Did you know vision boards are not only for manifesting yachts, mansions, and material things? You and your partner can create a vision board for your relationship so you can see what you're working towards and feel motivated to accomplish your vision. Follow these steps to create the vision board that encompasses your values, hopes, and dreams for your life together as a loving couple.

Step 1: What's the Purpose of Your Vision Board?

Be clear about what it is you'd like to accomplish in your relationship because that will determine what goes on the vision board. Do you want a relationship where you have more time with each other? Would you like to be more open and communicative about everything with no holds barred? The two of you need to brainstorm as a team and share values that the other person may not have mentioned or thought of. Make sure the goals you have for your relationship are clear and achievable so neither of you feels overwhelmed by trying to do too much all at once.

Step 2: Get the Materials for Your Vision Board.

You'll need a large piece of cardboard paper or a whiteboard if you prefer. While digital apps work well, having your vision board somewhere you can see each day is much better. So, if you're going the traditional route, you'll also need old magazines or posters and photos printed from the internet.

Step 3: Find the Images and Words That Match Your Goals.

You'll need to browse through magazines, online images, stills from movies, etc., to find every word and image that lines up beautifully with the goals you've set as a couple. You could also select stills of couples from your favorite movies that embody the sort of relationship you'd love to have with each other in real life, as they capture the spirit of the dream relationship— that you'll create with your significant other.

Step 4: Arrange the Printouts and Cutouts on the Board, Then Glue Them Down.

You should work together to make it look aesthetically pleasing to both of you and be willing to compromise when you don't see eye to eye. When you both take a step back and look at what you've done, and you're happy with the results, it's time to glue everything in place. Your vision board should be something you both love to look at.

Step 5: Set Your Board Somewhere You'll See It First Thing in the Morning and Last Thing at Night.

When you can see it every time you go to sleep and wake up, it will remind you of how deeply you value your relationship and the person you're so lucky to call your own. You'll be inspired to actively seek ways to reach your goals, and your intimacy with each other will be better and better each day.

Step 6: Please Check in with Each Other to Talk about How Well You're Doing.

You can't just set up a vision board, dust your hands, and expect some Law of Attraction fairy to wave magic dust all over it and make your dreams come true. There is work to be done, and you need to check in with each other to see how far along you've come since setting up the board. Try to check in at least once a week to see where you're doing better and what could use some improvement.

Chapter 6: Restoring Emotional and Physical Intimacy

One of the things that takes a massive hit from infidelity is intimacy. The betrayed partner has trouble letting the one who cheated close, physically or emotionally. As for the ones who cheated, they struggle with feelings of self-worth because of the guilt about what they've done, and not only that, in their bid to separate the person they cheated with from their significant other in their minds, they may not want to initiate any form of intimacy. On top of that, if your partner betrayed you, they're probably struggling because they expect you to reject any attempt they make to get close to you. You may already have rejected them in the heat of your anger — not that you're to be blamed for what's a natural, instinctual response to being cheated on.

Can intimacy be restored?
https://www.pexels.com/photo/man-and-woman-holding-hands-3228726/

So, the question is, can intimacy be restored? Is it possible to want to hold and be held by this person once more? Could you find it in yourself to be vulnerable with them and share your innermost thoughts as you used to do, once upon a time that feels so long ago it's almost like it was all a dream and nothing more? Well, you'll be glad to know that you can restore the intimate connection you once had and improve on it, too. That's what this chapter will teach you. You'll discover the secrets to bringing back the emotional and physical closeness you and your partner once had. You'll find an ember that can be nurtured into a bright, roaring fire if you can fan it just right.

The Effect of Infidelity on Emotional and Physical Intimacy

Infidelity hurts so much because of the havoc it wreaks on your emotional and physical well-being, and it also affects your ability to connect with your partner intimately in every way conceivable. First, here's a closer look at how infidelity affects how emotionally intimate you are with your partner. One undeniable effect is the pain of betrayal, making wanting anything to do with the person who was so willing to cause you such deep sadness unthinkable. When you realize you've been betrayed, nothing hurts more, and you trusted this person you once thought couldn't even be on the list of people who could hurt you. Your trust is gone, and, as a result, so is your desire to be intimate. Betrayal is a traumatic experience, and when you're traumatized, it's impossible to feel safe in general, let alone when you're facing the one who broke you.

The betrayal of infidelity causes every couple to become emotionally distant from each other, and sadly, you're no exception to the rule. It is natural to feel a sense of coldness at best or repulsion and disgust, at worst, toward your cheating partner. Sometimes, the feeling gets so bad that it devolves into outright resentment. If someone had told you in the weeks and months leading to the present time that you'd one day have the sort of hateful thoughts and feelings you do toward your partner, you would have laughed because the very idea would have been ridiculous. Yet, this is an unfortunate real effect of infidelity. It's impossible to build any emotional intimacy when, on the best of days, you feel cold, and on the worst of days, you're an unstoppable volcano desiring to burn everything about your partner.

When you can't be emotionally intimate with your partner, what are the odds you'll allow yourself to be physically intimate with them? It's impossible. Even if you tried, there would be a noticeable difference in the energy and purity of intimacy from before the unfaithful act happened compared to the present, after the fact. If you tried once, you'd not be willing to give it a go again because, somehow, you feel dirty. As for your partner, they're too riddled with the shame and guilt of their choices to be truly present with you. It's uncomfortable for you both because this third person between you, while not physically present, takes up so much space between you as though they're the elephant in the room.

When you learn you've been cheated on, you feel anxious, stressed, and depressed, and sometimes, your mental symptoms can get so bad that they play out as chronic pain and other physical ailments. The last thing on your mind is getting physically intimate, and if you have to take medication for your condition, guess what? You will most likely be disinclined to have your partner touch you in any way. You may also be unwilling because of your loss of self-esteem since the natural place your mind heads to when you're betrayed is that you must not have been good enough for your partner.

Obstacles on the Path to Restoring Emotional and Physical Intimacy

The following are obstacles you will have to contend with when you are on the journey of restoring the bond between you and your other half:

1. You may make yourself too busy, not realizing that's only to distract yourself from the problems at home.

2. You and your partner may give in to the temptation to criticize each other. Usually, whatever you're criticizing each other about has nothing to do with what's really going on. Your cutting looks and remarks are really a cry for help, a call for attention, a desire to end the madness you find yourselves hopelessly drowning in, silenced by egos too big to admit their pain or to be vulnerable.

3. Impatience is another problem, as you may be less willing to put up with things you had no trouble tolerating before things went south.

4. Your perception of yourself could make it hard to be willing to reach out to the other person and others in your life.

These are just some of the barriers that could be in the way when you decide to develop your emotional and physical intimacy. You have to be on the lookout for these obstacles and be proactive about dealing with them. Otherwise, they will leech whatever love is left between you and your partner, and it will only be a matter of time before your relationship ends.

Worksheet: Bringing Back Emotional and Physical Closeness

This exercise aims to help you and your partner create the best conditions to make it easier to reestablish and strengthen your intimacy.

Part 1: For Emotional Intimacy

1. You'll need a pen and paper for this one. Together, brainstorm various things you know you both enjoy doing as a couple. Don't feel the need to make every item on your list too fancy or ambitious. For instance, if you enjoy simple things like watching a movie together, you should add that to your list. What about walking or taking a hike? Is camping something you'd both be open to? You could also write things you've never done before as a couple or on your own and give them a go.

2. Set a schedule for when you'll do these activities, being mindful that you both need to be in the right headspace for them. It's best not to schedule things when the other person will be busy. Here's a list of things to help you get started (you can add more activities if you wish):

    a. Date nights (could be indoors or outdoors).

    b. Travel (you could go somewhere you've been together before or somewhere you've both never been but have always wanted to check out).

    c. Work out with each other. Make sure you choose something that matches both of your fitness levels.

    d. Make a meal together, whether it's something new and unfamiliar or something you're both good at.

    e. Volunteer your time to a cause you both care about. You could go to an animal shelter, for instance.

  f. Take a class on something you've both been meaning to learn.

3. After each activity, take time to think about how you feel about each other. Is there any change? Are you any closer? Write about your feelings in your journal, then share your thoughts. If you don't feel closer to the other person, don't be dishonest. Tell the truth with kindness. Also, if it turns out it's your partner who doesn't feel any positive change, you shouldn't be mad at them. Change takes time. Be patient and trust the process.

Part 2: For Physical Intimacy

Remember, you can't fast-forward your way from broken intimacy to sex. It doesn't work like that. For now, your focus should be on non-sexual touches. So, keep that in mind as you do this next part of the worksheet.

1. You have to have a heart-to-heart conversation about how you both feel regarding getting physically intimate with one another. Among the critical matters you should discuss are your boundaries. What are you comfortable with? What isn't, okay? You need to know these things about your partner, too. As always, there's no reason to rush this process. It will take as long as it needs to.

2. Come to an agreement about the physical touch you're willing to start with. Perhaps you could manage a ten-second hug or at least hold hands for a minute. What's the point? It's to teach your bodies and minds that there's nothing to be afraid of when touching each other, to remind yourselves that once upon a time, you couldn't stand being apart and that you really do miss that. Do this daily rather than wait for the "perfect" occasion to connect. You could do this right before you go to bed, as this will help you keep your goal of restoring intimacy in your mind while you sleep. The result is it will be the first thing on your mind when you wake up, and whether you know it or not, you'll seek ways to show each other more affection. Other ideas besides hugging and holding hands include cuddling, offering each other non-sexual massages, reassuring squeezes, rubs, and pats.

3. At the end of each day, write in your journal what it felt like to be connected. Have you realized that what you interpreted as disgust or repulsion is a thin veneer for the danger you felt? Are you

learning more and more that there's nothing dangerous about the other person's trust? Are you starting to get that warm glow in your heart yet? Don't worry if this doesn't happen the first week or even a month of doing this exercise. Keep going, and you'll see progress eventually.

Worksheet: Conversational Prompts

1. **What Are Your Dreams?** What do you hope to accomplish? Talk about it with each other. Share where you think you'll be in five to ten years. Be willing to be vulnerable, and never miss a moment to find your sense of humor.

2. **Now, What Are Your Fears?** What are the things that keep you up at night, your insecurities, and concerns? Listen actively and empathetically to each other, as this is a great opportunity to connect on a deeply emotional level.

3. **How Did Your Day Go?** Talk about it with each other. Listen to each other because this shouldn't be about one person stealing the show. Let each person shine. Celebrate good news, and empathize over the bad. This is how you'll connect better emotionally and, eventually, physically.

4. **Share Memories of Childhood.** Think about your favorite ones and your darkest ones. Share it all, and hold nothing back. As you do, you'll not only learn new things about each other but also have a better understanding of why you each act the way you do.

5. **Talk about the Things That Mean the Most to You**, as in the things you value the most in life, as this is another way to find common ground with each other and learn how to meet each other halfway.

6. **Next, Talk about the Things You Love the Most about Each Other.** What was it that drew you to each other? Talk about the funny things you noticed about each other in a good-natured way so there's something to laugh about. Laughing is an excellent way to strengthen your bond as a couple.

7. **Now, Talk about What You Love about Your Relationship** and what you think you could make better with a little more attention and elbow grease.

Exploring Touch Further

Touch is such a powerful way to connect with someone else. There are many ways to touch each other that don't have to do with sex but will help bring you closer to each other and show you can trust each other once more. People underestimate the range of emotions and messages that can be communicated with a simple touch. Touch your partner one way, and it shows them gratitude. Change it up a bit, and you're showing them you're feeling vulnerable. Make another adjustment, and you're offering comfort or reassurance. Done lackadaisically, it communicates a lack of concern.

So, what does non-sexual touch look like? It's putting an arm over the other person's shoulder, stroking their neck or back as you pass them, or holding their hand. It's touching your partner on the face, softly, to show them how precious they are to you. It's touching their arm gently to show your support and empathy. Whatever you choose, when you add eye contact into the mix, you exponentially increase the love and care behind those sweet gestures, tugging on the other person's emotional heartstrings while reminding yourself why you've chosen this person rather than anyone else to do this "life" thing with.

Eye contact can increase the emotion behind gestures.
https://unsplash.com/photos/woman-in-black-sleeveless-dress-lying-on-green-grass-field-0eErMhzFgvE?utm_content=creditShareLink&utm_medium=referral&utm_source=unsplash

How can you use touch to show your partner you care about them? You could offer them a foot massage when they're tired or just because. It's great for them as they'll feel relaxed as you touch them. A hand massage is also lovely to receive, and you can do this while you're watching a movie or being "alone together" while you're both doing your own thing in the same room. You could also hold them close, as this will feel comforting and increases oxytocin, a hormone that encourages bonding. It's called the "love hormone" for a good reason, which is why you should both hold each other for a minute or more a day to boost your trust in each other and stop being afraid. As you hold each other, your hypothalamus generates oxytocin, which tells you both that you're safe.

Did you know that when you hold each other, you also create other hormones like dopamine and serotonin? Well, why do they matter? Dopamine is called the "reward hormone," and it's the reason you're ready to work hard on something until you accomplish it. It's the reason you feel good. So, as you hug each other, you feel happy, and you'll want to touch each other more often. Naturally, this will spill over, causing you both to be more willing to be emotionally intimate. Your brain registers touch between you two as a good thing to be sought out as often as possible. Then there's the serotonin, or the "happy hormone," which is excellent for keeping your mood nice and steady. Holding each other in a tender embrace encourages your brain to release serotonin, making you feel true happiness. It feels like your body and mind are at their best, and you're both in a better position to connect.

Don't be afraid to use touch to show your partner you care if they're open to it, whether it's a cuddle, a hair ruffle, or a gentle kiss on the cheek or the forehead. You have to be attentive, too, so if you can tell they don't want to be touched, you let them be and allow them to come to you. Do you know what's even better? Asking for consent before you touch your partner. Sure, it's easy to assume that's not necessary because you're not touching them sexually, but by asking for consent, you show your partner you care about them. Also, asking shows them you're willing to be vulnerable, encouraging them to do the same with you. If there's one thing to always remember, it's this. The small gestures make the most significant changes in restoring your emotional and physical intimacy with each other. Set your ego aside, wear your heart on your sleeve, talk with each other about your action plan to restore your closeness, and don't be afraid to give it your all.

Chapter 7: Sexual Intimacy and Reconciliation

Now that you've made progress on restoring emotional and physical intimacy in your relationship, it's time to address the matter of sexual intimacy. It's going to take time and effort to get to the point where you and your partner enjoy being sexual with each other, but you can pull it off. There's no shortcut through this process. It's going to take as long as necessary. If either of you feel rushed, it will only slow things down, increase the awkwardness and discomfort, and possibly put you off the idea of sexual intimacy altogether. At this point, you need to use open communication and mutual respect as your best tools to bring back the spark between you both. Before you can conquer the challenge of a dead bedroom, you need to know how you got here in the first place. You need to know everything about how infidelity destroys sexual intimacy to reverse-engineer the process.

Open communication and mutual respect can bring back the spark between you and your partner.
https://www.pexels.com/photo/photo-of-a-man-being-hugged-4406725/

The Impact of Infidelity on Sexual Intimacy

An Unwillingness to be Sexually Intimate Because of Guilt: If your partner's the one who cheated, they'll have a hard time wanting to be intimate with you for several reasons, chief of them being they don't think you've forgiven them. So, they prefer not to even try. They are being eaten up from the inside by the shame of choosing betrayal over keeping your relationship. When this is what's happening, they can't even allow themselves to be emotionally intimate with you or have conversations about your feelings. If you try to initiate sex, they'll be hesitant. They can't be in the moment because they're stuck in their head, wondering how and why you could still be with them, fearful that they'll wind up pushing you away if they say or do the wrong thing. They may not even be aware of all that is happening in their minds, and, in that case, they may not even have the libido to see things through, let alone be turned on enough to want to share a bed.

A Feeling of Numbness: From the moment you learn your partner has cheated on you, a part of you dies. Everything about you that enjoyed feeling pleasure shuts down, not just in your mind but in your body as well. The reason this happens is because the discovery of infidelity is a form of trauma, and trauma always leaves its mark on body, mind, and spirit. So, when you first discover the truth and the reality of the situation hits you fully, you're in shock. Your body thinks that's because you're in trouble, so to protect you, it shuts down. It's like you get a hit of natural Novocain, and you're numb now, both emotionally and physically, which means you don't react or respond as you ordinarily would to anything, let alone sexual touch. The numbness affects every sense organ, and that includes your skin. Your partner can't look, smell, or feel good enough to get you sexually excited. Their touch doesn't do it for you anymore, and you'd rather not bother with even the most non-sexual of touches.

A Desire to Guard Your Partner: When you discover betrayal, you may become so anxious about your partner that you begin to act territorially around them, doing all you can to signal to others that they're yours and everyone needs to back off. This isn't romantic behavior, as the movies would have you believe. Instead, your desire to give in to "mate guarding" is a primal one driven by raw fear and anxiety rather than a need to bring back the love between you. By acting this way, you signal to your partner that you don't trust them not to slip up again, whether you mean to or not. This makes them feel even more ashamed and unlikely to want to engage with you sexually.

Even if you have sex with them, you'll both be able to tell it's not coming from a place of genuine desire for each other but that there's a cloud of desperation hanging over both of you. They'll also feel they're only consenting to your advances because they feel pressured. All of this causes your relationship to buckle under the weight of all these fear-driven expectations as your partner begins to resent you, even if you feel they don't have the right to since they cheated. You can see how none of this does your relationship any favors.

Intense Trust Issues: The breach of trust from betrayal makes it hard for you to want to open up or put yourself in a vulnerable position with your betrayer by allowing them access to your body. In a relationship, you expect your partner to protect and preserve your emotional safety, but then, once unfaithfulness enters the picture, it's close to impossible to open yourself up like that. You're mistrustful – and with good reason. The thought of putting yourself in a position to be fooled once more is a huge turn-off, and even when you really want to let it go, it's tough. You'll need time to recover, to break down the barrier between you and your partner that keeps you from sharing your love and affection for each other freely, without shame or guilt.

There's also the risk that even after you've forgiven your partner, they may have trouble trusting that you've let it all go. So, whether consciously or not, they punish themselves by refusing to give themselves to you fully when you're attempting to connect with them emotionally and sexually. They don't trust that you're sincere in your desire to be with them physically. They're watching you through eyes squinting in suspicion as they wait for the other shoe to drop or for the mask they imagine you're wearing to slip.

The Natural Ebb and Flow of Sexual Desire

You're human, and one of the key traits of humanity is having desires, with sexual desire being one of the most basic and important ones. It's about wanting to connect or bond with someone else through the wonderful gift of sex, and unless in an asexual relationship, it's expected that you and your partner will connect with each other this way. Sexual desire is a fundamental part of conventional relationships, determining how long your union with your partner will last. It's about more than just physical pleasure, allowing you and your partner to enjoy the feeling of loving and being loved.

The level of sexual desire is not the same all the time, as it ebbs and flows for everyone, and it's natural for you and your partner not to be as sexually active as you were with each other at the start of your relationship. You may both be advancing in years. Or, one or both of you may struggle with more stress than usual. If there's been a significant change or upheaval in your routine, sex may be the last thing on your mind, and the same applies when there are serious health issues that need to be addressed. You should never let anyone make you feel your relationship is on the rocks because you and your partner aren't going at it like bunnies. It's only natural for the dynamics between you to wax and wane with time. However, when you're not having sex because of infidelity, that's a different matter entirely and one that needs to be addressed. Infidelity can take the ebb and flow and turn it stagnant with no action at all. A dead bedroom could lead to the end of the relationship if you don't do the work to bring back sexual intimacy.

Body and Heart

There's an undeniable connection between emotional intimacy and sexual intimacy in the context of a marriage or a relationship. You can't experience sexual intimacy without there being an emotional connection. If you want to enjoy better sex, you have to work on strengthening the emotional bonds you share, and the more you connect sexually, the stronger your feelings for each other will become. Your bodies and hearts are intricately connected.

Think back to when you and your partner began to realize you were falling for each other. If you consider things carefully, you'll realize the first thing that happened was that you became emotionally vulnerable with each other, having lost your fear of being criticized, mocked, judged, or silenced for being your authentic self. The first time you got naked with each other, you still had your clothes on. How's that possible? You bared your hearts to each other. You said to each other, "Hey, this is all of me, no frills, no masks, and no costumes." From this position, you can create a powerful relationship where you understand and value each other.

Right now, things may not be looking good on the sexual front, but it is possible to sort that out, especially if you've begun working to restore your emotional intimacy by using the exercises from the previous chapter.

Worksheet: Understanding Your Desires and Boundaries

There are a few steps you have to take before you and your partner can be warmed up enough to try sexual intimacy and continue the process of building it. Both of you must do some self-reflection to find out exactly what you need from the other person sexually and what boundaries you have that you'd prefer to be respected. The purpose of this particular worksheet is to encourage self-reflection regarding your sexual desires. Answer the following questions honestly and in as much detail as you can manage in your journal, and discuss your answers with each other when you've finished. This worksheet is a powerful tool to help you and your significant other communicate openly and constructively about these essential matters that hold the key to reigniting the passion between you.

Part 1: Reflecting on Your True Desires

1. When you reflect on your needs and desires in the bedroom, what are the things you love to do that make you feel satisfied?

2. What emotions would you rather feel to help you get in the mood and appreciate the afterglow?

3. Do you have specific preferences, dos and don'ts, and fantasies that you feel would make a sexual connection with your partner more satisfying?

4. Consider every sexual experience you've had in the past, whether with your partner or someone else. Now you have these experiences in mind, what was it about them that you enjoyed, and what do you think you could do to make them happen with your partner?

5. Still recalling your most memorable sexual experiences, what did you hate about them? Is there anything that reminds you of those cringe or uncomfortable moments when you're with your partner sexually? How can you communicate with your partner to stop those things or reach a compromise if your partner gets off on them?

Part 2: Discovering, Clarifying, and Communicating Boundaries

1. What are some of the activities you and your partner have been engaged in sexually in the past that make you feel uncomfortable? List them all, and if you can explain why, do so. If not, that's fine, too.

2. What sort of behavior or sexual activity is an absolute no-no for you?

3. What could your partner do to make you feel like they truly value and respect you before, during, and after your sexual connection?

4. What are some concerning things from your past sexual encounters with your partner (or someone else) that have you worried or afraid, unable to be in the moment and enjoy yourself?

5. What are the things that trigger you badly, whether it's something said or done? List them, and if you'd like to go into detail on each point, do so.

Nurturing a Safe and Intimate Space for Sexual Intimacy

The safer you and your partner feel with each other, the more likely it will be that you'll develop sexual intimacy once more. Remember, you can only be sexually intimate with your partner if both of you are willing to put yourselves in vulnerable positions. However, it is tough to be vulnerable when you feel threatened. So, the point of the following exercises is to help you feel more at ease exploring each other 's bodies and ideas around sexuality. First, here's a look at the many advantages of taking time to create an environment that feels safe for you.

Your willingness to be vulnerable makes it easier to forgive. Your partner will open up as you communicate through words and actions that it is safe to be with you. You, in turn, will be touched by their willingness to be vulnerable. From this space, you can be more honest about your feelings. Even when you assume you've been doing a good job of letting go of the resentment and pain you feel every time you think about your partner and what they did, you may be surprised to find a few sneaky demons are left haunting your thoughts. From this place of safety, you'll be surprised to find the actual insecurities responsible for the few moments when you slip up and say something cutting or feel terrible about this other person. The moments these truths come to light, you can let them go, and you'll be delighted to discover a newer level of closeness with your partner.

Pleasure boosts the speed at which you regain your trust in each other. As you discover the delight of touching each other and feel the warmth that floods your chest as you remember how your partner knows exactly what you like, you'll feel encouraged to trust them more. When you respond to your partner's touch, you make them feel more confident that you love them, and they realize what you share is very precious. Physical and sexual intimacy are about giving and receiving. When it's obvious to each of you that you do want to give the other person pleasure and you would appreciate the pleasure they offer you, you are spurred on to break down any other walls that may still be between you two. Sex is a spiritual act that causes two souls to become one in the moment, and there is no way to let that happen without trust. It is the ultimate act of vulnerability between couples.

You can share the things words can't convey. The truth about emotions, especially in the context of a relationship that is clawing its way back from the abyss it's been plunged into by infidelity, is that they are far too deep and complex to be expressed with words. So, as you work together to create an environment that feels safe and will encourage intimacy, you'll find yourself sharing things that no words could adequately capture. It may sound a little woo-woo, but it is a real thing that you can communicate with each other by simply sitting in silence together. Add in the element of touch and sensuality, and you will increase the volume of the message you're passing along to each other. What's the result? You develop new depths of emotional connection, making it impossible to sever yourselves from each other.

As you communicate with each other in this safe space, your sensuality grows. When your relationship is hit with infidelity, you'll find you no longer feel connected to your partner and are unwilling to explore your sensual side with them, or anyone else for that matter. The way to fix this is to be in a safe space to share your thoughts, feelings, and, eventually, bodies with each other freely. You'll become incredibly sensual once more, and if you make a point of affirming each other by saying things like, "I really like that," or "I love it every time you..." you'll watch your sensuality boom, the walls between you crash, and your hearts blend to become one.

You'll find yourselves desiring each other again. It's one thing to wait for your partner to initiate sexual contact and then respond to it. It's another thing entirely to be unable to wait for them and seek them out yourself. That's what will happen when you both put in the work to create a safe, nurturing space to explore sexual intimacy with each other once more. The more you do it, the more you'll be rewarded with oxytocin, serotonin, and dopamine, and you'll naturally seek out your partner to continue to get a fix. Now, talking about what happens from a chemical perspective is not the most romantic thing on the planet, but if you keep your focus on how that chemical process plays out behaviorally, you'll find that it's worth putting in the time to become hopelessly bound to each other once more, desperate to feel one another every chance you get and, in every way, possible.

You'll develop emotional safety with each other, which is a signal that you're sexually liberated with each other. The problem with the anxiety and insecurity that comes after infidelity is that you and your partner will have a massive problem with spontaneously expressing yourself. If in the past you had no trouble giving one another spontaneous hugs, kisses, and "love taps" on your behinds as you pass by, you now find yourself having to hold back. So, as you develop a safe space where you can communicate honestly and genuinely show each other how hurt you are and how much you want to fix things, you will eventually find yourselves feeling emotionally safe. You'll experience that safety in the bedroom. You'll feel liberated. You'll be willing to do things that, in the past, you probably never thought you could ever do again. So, as you approach the process of rebuilding your sexual intimacy from this state of emotional security, you will find yourselves being willing to explore with no embarrassment. Nothing is more joyful than being spontaneous and free to know that no one will judge you for your choices or what you like. This is why taking the time to set the tone is essential.

Sensory Reconnection Exercise

After you and your partner have chosen a time and space where you know you won't be interrupted (freeing you to let things progress naturally), you must begin by reminding yourself what *feeling each other is like.* That means you have to awaken your senses. The point of this exercise is to help you and your partner find your bond once more through your sensory perception. You can't just rush right into having sex with each other after you've experienced such a rip between you. By slowly exploring each other and titillating your senses, you can gradually reintroduce the idea of safety and security to the bedroom.

Instructions

Gather some materials to help you and your partner explore your senses. Here are a few things you should consider:

1. For **audio,** you'll need to have a speaker and a playlist prepared. It's best to choose a genre of music you both enjoy that will encourage a romantic, soft mood.

2. For **smell,** get perfumes, essential oils, scented candles, and bath bombs. Check to ensure the essential oils are dermatologically tested and skin-friendly.

3. For **sight,** you should both choose to wear something appealing, and you can decorate the space you'll be in with flowers, special lighting, or whatever else can make the place look aesthetically pleasing.

4. Get massage oils, feathers, and soft materials like silk or velvet for **touch.**

5. You'll need some beverages (something you both like), fruit, and snacks for **taste.**

Pick somewhere comfy and safe. If you have kids, it's best to have them be elsewhere for the time being, or you may want to plan a getaway to somewhere special. Set up the room so it's cozy and intimate to focus on each other without distractions. Wherever you are, set everything you need in place so there's no need to keep trooping out of the room to get one thing or another. You want to avoid being unprepared so the mood isn't ruined.

Begin by breathing deeply. You don't have to do fancy meditation if you're unfamiliar with the process. First, sit opposite each other. Then, each of you must pay attention to your breathing for a few minutes. When it's clear you're both settled and in the moment, turn your attention to the other person's breathing. You may find your breathing patterns synchronize with each other's. This is a good thing.

First, explore hearing. You can put your playlist on. As you listen to the music, you should take turns describing what the sounds feel like. Music always evokes emotion, so this shouldn't be a problem. Suppose you struggle to find the right emotions. In that case, it's okay to describe the song as a color, an element of weather like the rain, sun, or a typhoon, an experience like a baby's laugh or a first kiss, etc. Do this for a few songs, then listen to each other's voices. Listen to what you love about each other's voice, and complement each other, keeping eye contact as you do. Then, you may listen to more songs or check in with each other to see if you're ready to move on to the next step.

Move on to smell. You can allow the music to keep playing (hopefully, your playlist is a long one, and if it isn't, you've put it on a loop to start over when it's done) while you bring out each of the things you've chosen for the smell sensory experience. Take turns smelling each scent, and talk about how they make you feel, affect your mood, what or who they remind you of, etc. Sometimes, smells will hit you differently after a second or third check, so be willing to breathe them in again to truly understand what the other person is sharing with you about how the smell affects them. When you've finished experiencing all the smells, move closer to each other and try to pick up on every scent you can, from cologne to aftershave, to perfumes and oils, to natural musk. Take it all in without saying anything for a while, and then when you're ready, share with the other person what you appreciate about their smell, whether it's the comfort you get from its familiarity or something else. Ensure you hold eye contact as you talk about this.

Move on to the visuals. You can start by taking in the things you've brought to make the room visually pleasing. Talk about how you feel about them, taking turns to share your thoughts and asking questions where you'd like clarification. Become curious about the other person's perspective. Then, when you've finished looking at everything else, it's time to focus on the other person.

Take each other in, noticing everything from how your partner's dressed to how they've styled their hair and accessorized, as well as how the colors they've chosen suit them. Offer each other genuine compliments about what you can visually appreciate about each other, keeping eye contact and smiling softly at each other. If you've been taking your time with the exercise so far, you should feel familiar warmth for the other person in your heart.

Now it's time to play with touch. You can start by picking one of the objects you've brought for exploring touch. Feel that item with your hands or against your face, then describe how it feels to your partner. Have them do the same thing with you. You can use these items to touch the other person, avoiding direct skin contact for now. At this point, ask each other if they notice a difference between when they felt the material alone and when you used it to touch them.

When you finish each item, it's time to touch each other. Reach out and hold hands while keeping your gaze locked on the other person's eyes. Don't move your hands right away. Simply keep their hands in yours. As you hold hands, take turns describing the other person's hands, from texture to temperature, pressure, etc. Then, take turns describing your emotions as you hold each other's hands, focusing on the present. After a while, you can move on to gently rubbing each other's hands, still describing your feelings and any beautiful memories that well up in your mind. Play with the speed and pressure; be playful, be gentle.

Don't thumb your nose at this: Try to emote with your hands. Imagine you're sending your partner a feeling of love and appreciation through your hands to theirs and their heart. Don't think about what that will look like. Instead, allow your hands to do what they will. They know how to pass the message along. You can also smile or gaze lovingly at the other person before you tell them you appreciate them for being so committed to your relationship that they're here, with you, doing this exercise.

If you're both feeling up to it, you can check in with each other to see if you're both open to hugging and holding each other. There's nothing sexual going on here, at least, not yet, and not if you're both not feeling up to it. However, don't be surprised to find that you both have a ravenous desire to be close to each other in every way imaginable at this point in the exercise. If you can turn the lights down lower, that's great. If not, don't sweat it. Just bask in the feeling of being in each other's arms, listening to the music, smelling your combined scents, taking in the moment visually, and being in the here and now with your forever person.

There's no stopping now if you both sense a desire for more intimacy, whether through kisses, caresses, or something more. Surrender to the beauty of being vulnerable with another human, of rediscovering your love and trust for each other once more. It's a rebirth of your love. Nothing from the past exists. This is a new first for you both, one that leads to a glorious life full of love, laughter, light, and joy. If you're not keen on connecting sexually yet, that's fine, too. You could also take turns massaging each other. That's why you have the oil, isn't it? Try to keep it non-sexual unless you both desire more and consent to taking things to the next level. Being consistent with this exercise will eventually lead you both to a place of safety and willingness to try again. The fact that you've both arrived at this point is still causing you to hope for better and, eventually, celebrate your newfound spark.

Now, experiment with taste. Take turns describing the foods, snacks, and whatever else to each other. It's okay not to be fond of how something tastes. Be honest in sharing and describing the food (and please be kind if your significant other took the time to prepare it). This is a chance to have fun, unwind, and enjoy yourselves.

It's time to reflect on how this exercise made you feel. What was it like for you? Take turns sharing, and while you're at it, address the matter of feeling connected and safe with each other, even if it's only been for these few moments. Talk about how to make this a ritual (how often will you do this, during what times, at what location, etc.), and brainstorm ideas to make the next session more interesting.

Finally, thank each other. Let the other person know how much you appreciate their willingness to try to reclaim the relationship. Thank them for choosing to be here rather than anywhere else and fully present with you. They should also tell you how much they appreciate your time and effort. As you wrap up your thanks, verbally commit to making this happen and let the other person know you're looking forward to the next session. Also, plan to bring one "surprise" element to the next one so you both have something to look forward to. It doesn't have to be something elaborate. It only needs to be interesting. This is your chance to break down walls because whatever you choose could have a humorous, revealing, and vulnerable backstory, bringing you closer to each other than ever.

21 Conversational Prompts to Elevate Your Sexual Intimacy

Do you want to be clear about your sexual needs with your partner? Want to know what they'd love from you? How would you like to establish firm, unquestionable boundaries that make you respect each other even more and fall even deeper in love as a result? Use the following prompts. Get ready to be emotionally naked with each other as you answer.

1. "How did infidelity affect the way you feel about the sexual connection we have with each other?"

2. "What can I do to help you feel safer and give you confidence in our love and sexual relationship?"

3. "Is there something I do or say that you'd rather I didn't because they make you remember terrible things from the past or leave you feeling awkward and uncomfortable?"

4. "Do you have any idea how we could have even more trust and vulnerability in the sexual aspect of our relationship with each other?"

5. "Are there better ways we can let each other know what we need and want from each other sexually?"

6. "Can we come up with boundaries for both of us that will always help us feel safe and satisfied with each other in our sexual interactions?"

7. "Are there some things you'd love to try sexually and things you'd rather steer clear of? Please share."

8. "In what ways can we keep our sexual relationship feeling like it's safe for each person and as a couple?"

9. "Do you have any idea how we can encourage a deeper physical and emotional connection between each other? Please share."

10. "Would you be open to working with a professional, like a therapist or a counselor, to help us maneuver our way to deeper levels of sexual intimacy?"

11. "What ideas do you have for staying honest and open with each other about our feelings, thoughts, and experiences of our sexual relationship from now on?"

12. "In what ways is our sexual relationship different from how it used to be before it got hit with infidelity?"

13. "What ideas do you have for how we can keep our sexual relationship fresh, fun, invigorating, and satisfying?"

14. "What do you honestly feel each time we are sexually intimate with each other?"

15. "What things turn you on the most each time we make love, whether it's a specific word or something we do?"

16. "When we're sexually intimate, what makes you feel comforted and loved?"

17. "Do you have any ideas on how we can give our sexual relationship a higher priority than we have in the past? Please share your thoughts."

18. "Could you tell me what I can do to make you feel deeply desired and wanted?"

19. "Outside the context of sex, in what ways can I demonstrate my love and affection for you?"

20. "What are your genuine thoughts about how sexually connected and intimate we are with each other?"

21. "What strategies can we put in place to fan the flames of our sexual connection so it burgeons stronger and better with time?"

Other Activities for Developing Sexual Intimacy

The following are excellent things to incorporate into your love life right away to see the sparks fly and your hunger for each other become powerfully unstoppable.

1. **Read Erotic Literature Together**. Not a fan of reading? No problem. You can both listen to erotic audiobooks. Are you both fancy with words? How about writing some of your own erotica, which you can read to each other? At best, you'll turn each other on. At worst, you'll have a good laugh over any ridiculous bits. If you're laughing, please keep it good-natured. If you're the one being teased, please have a sense of humor and take it in good spirits. Play is a lovely segue to sex, you know.

2. **Groom Each Other** — no, not like cats, unless you're trying to get a laugh or that's your thing. You could share shower time with each other, helping each other clean up. This is a lovely way to be close to each other, and there's no better demonstration of care than literally caring for the other person's body.

3. **Share Your Fantasies.** Then, see how you can make them come true. You have to be tender and respectful of each other here because often, people feel vulnerable about talking about these things. So, you and your partner should declare your space a safe zone where you can talk about these things without fear. Go the extra mile by seeing how you can please each other unless engaging in said fantasy would breach your boundaries. In that case, you can come to a workable agreement with each other.

4. When you're sexually intimate with each other, **Use Your Words and Body Language to Encourage Each Other.** Do this, especially when your partner does something you like. Also, check in with each other the whole time. You're making love, which means it's not about getting yours and getting done. It's about fulfilling the other person's needs, too.

5. **Switch up the Locations** where you both get intimate with each other. Novelty is great for reigniting dying embers every time. Speaking of novelty, what else can you switch up?

6. **Don't Shy Away from Accessories, Props, and Toys** — unless you find them highly uncomfortable or triggering. Don't let your unfamiliarity with these things keep you from trying them out. You may like some things and laugh at others, but either way, they can make things more fun and exciting for you and your lover.

7. **Earn an Oscar — by Role-Playing.** You and your partner can embody other characters to bring back the mystery and excitement between you. Discuss this before you attempt to be someone else for the day or night because your partner may not catch on or be in the mood. It's also good to let them know because you could both develop backstories and scripts for the characters you'll assume. Set a day and a time for this, as well as a signal for when you both know you're done with acting. While it's role-playing, it should be taken seriously. If one of you keeps slipping out of character, it could kill the mood or make things feel too absurd for you to enjoy yourselves. You can have all the laughs you want with

each other after the night is over. For fun, you could award each other makeshift Oscars after.

Before moving on from this chapter, please remember you and your partner need to be patient with each other as you work through your sexual intimacy issues. Keep your hearts and minds open. What can you do when you feel a strong push against opening yourself up to your partner? Stay curious. When you think you don't want to engage, pause to ask yourself, "Do I really not want to? Why?" This is how you determine the subconscious blocks to sexual intimacy that stop you from letting that wall crumble. Talk to your partner about it, and see how you can convince yourself to at least be curious about the process (while respecting all boundaries, yours and your partner's). If you approach the process of bringing back the spark with curiosity, your heart and mind will be less defensive.

Chapter 8: Extra Tips for a Positive Outcome

By this point in the book, you should be feeling optimistic about your prospects. You should know that it is possible to revive your relationship and make it even better than it was in the beginning. This chapter aims to give you even more tips that will increase the chances of a positive outcome for your relationship. It is not impossible for you to be in love with this person again and be willing to share your heart, body, and soul with them. All you need is to commit to the process of rescuing your relationship from the jaws of infidelity. You both have to put in effort and support each other because you won't always feel like you can pull it off. During those times, what will help you pull through is a little more patience and understanding. Once you both accept that you can give your relationship a second wind, you are more than halfway through the battle.

The goal is to share your heart, body, and soul with your partner.
https://www.pexels.com/photo/goal-lettering-text-on-black-background-5598296/

Tips for Setting Positive and Realistic Intentions

An excellent way to ensure that you will achieve your goal of recovering your relationship is by keeping your intentions positive and also rooting them in reality. While it is good to hope for the best, you must be realistic about what you can accomplish within any time frame. The human heart is a complicated thing, and so is the mind, so it would be unfair and unrealistic of you to put a time limit on your partner, expecting them to recover within that period. It would also be unfair to yourself. With that out of the way, as long as you both remain committed to the cause, you will achieve progress.

If you want to improve the odds of recovery, you should reframe the process by thinking of it as a never-ending journey of love and dedication to each other. There is no endpoint to this process because there isn't any point at which you love someone "enough" and, therefore, no longer have to show your love. Love, in the context of a relationship, is meant to be a lifelong commitment, so if you are looking at rebuilding after infidelity through this lens, you should have no trouble remaining committed. The correct answer to "How long will this take?" is forever, or at least for as long as you intend to remain together as a couple. So, how can you set the best intentions for your connection, keeping them positive and achievable?

As individuals, find out what your core values are. Core values are everything that you hold in high esteem in life. These are the things that drive you. They inform your boundaries and motivate you to make things happen. These values are non-negotiable. Otherwise, they wouldn't be core values. Take time to reflect on your life and discover the things that you hold dear. When you know what matters to you, you and your partner can get together and see how your values align with each other's. After finding the synergy between both perspectives, you can use your newfound knowledge to drive your intentions and actions toward restoring and growing your relationship. Since you'll both be acting based on your inner values, there is a lower chance of doing anything to jeopardize your union ever again. You'll be proactive about keeping your relationship healthy and happy.

Go beyond simply fixing your connection. Remember, your relationship is meant to last for as long as you're together, which, if you're like normal couples, is for all the time you both have together on earth. In that case, you shouldn't only be looking for how to patch up the holes in your relationship. Your drive should be towards creating a future you can both look forward to enjoying together. If you are only committed to fixing the damage that has been caused by infidelity, you risk stagnating your relationship. Once you attain that goal, there's nothing further to aspire to, and that could be a recipe for disaster. Another reason you should reach for something loftier than mere repair is if you shoot for the moon and miss, you will at least land among the stars. In other words, you will do more than repair your relationship since you'd have to have sorted that out already before you can accomplish the goal of growing as a couple and loving each other more as time passes.

Worksheet: Powerful Intentions for Real Results

Use this worksheet to help you and your partner figure out the things that matter to you the most so you have a better shot at healing your connection after infidelity and doing even more than that.

Part 1: Value and Vision

1. Write down five or ten of your core values in your journal. These values should be centered on your relationships and life in general. For instance, you may value loyalty, openness, honesty, intimacy, communication, etc.

2. Pause for a few minutes to consider the way infidelity affected your perception of your values and how you see yourself. Then, note your observations in your journal.

3. Take some time to think about the future you would love to have regarding your relationship with your partner while working your core values in the mix. Then, as honestly as you can, write about what you desire from your relationship with your partner in the future.

4. From a place of sincerity, fully commit yourself to fixing your relationship and then some. Write about your dedication to the cause. To give your commitment more potency, list at least three things you will do for yourself for the sake of your relationship.

Part 2: The Connecting Thread between Intentions

1. Share your list of core values with each other, and then talk about them. Find the places where you see them connect and where they diverge. Then, talk about how you can compromise with the values that differ (unless these values are clearly on opposite ends of the spectrum, in which case things won't work out), and use your common values to grow your relationship.

2. Now, share the vision that you both have for your future as a couple. The goal of this conversation is to look for the ways in which you see things the same and build on those commonalities.

3. Put your thinking caps on and figure out goals that are attainable and measurable, which will ultimately lead you to the vision that you have for your relationship in the future. Please note that as you make these plans, you must also consider each individual's goals.

4. Discuss your perceptions of what makes communication honest and open. When you have finished, you both have to draw up a plan to encourage this honesty to help your relationship become all it can be.

Worksheet: Finding Gems and Fortifying Your Fortress

Every relationship has its strengths. If you can find yours and build on them, you make it easier to recover your healthy, loving selves once more. Use this worksheet to help you find the good and fortify your love for each other.

Part 1: The Gems You Share

1. Do this step individually. You each have to come up with at least five (at most, ten) experiences you've had with your partner that you cherish the most. You should also write five to ten qualities you think are admirable about your relationship.

2. Swap lists with each other. After going through the other person's lists, take turns talking about each entry. Your goal is to discuss this in a celebratory way so you can both appreciate that you have something beautiful going on here.

3. Then, take turns talking about unique obstacles and challenges you've experienced and have triumphed over as a couple. A good

talking point would be how these obstacles somehow revealed the strengths and positives you carried within you as individuals and couples.

Part 2: Fortifying Your Love

1. As a team, revisit your list of strengths and positives, and choose three to five of the ones you deem most important to developing a healthy relationship that stands the test of time.

2. Next, you both have to brainstorm. What new habits can you start to help these strengths become even stronger? Are there certain things you can do right away and consistently to make these positive pillars of your relationship even more prominent and secure?

3. Discuss the issues you think could stand in the way of your love becoming stronger – honestly and openly. Get it all on paper. When you've done that, you have to come together and strategize ways to keep these weak links in your relationship from breaking on you and ruining what you've built so far.

4. Now it's time to consider how you will both be supportive of each other when the storms of life hit your relationship. Talk about how you handle everything from disagreements to pressure from the outside, from health issues to financial ones, etc.

5. The next step is to schedule time every week or month when you check in with each other to see how you're progressing on the journey of developing a stormproof relationship. Commit to showing up for each other during these check-ins and implementing the action plans you come up with each time.

6. Thank each other for participating in this exercise as a team and following through with the homework you've received.

Why You Need Constant Self-Reflection and Personal Growth

In any relationship, if one or both parties don't bother with self-reflection and do anything to achieve personal growth, that relationship is doomed to fail. Two people make up this union, and to achieve the heights it can, both must be proactive about becoming better versions of themselves. How can you become a better version of yourself if you don't take the time to reflect on your choices and your current position in life so far?

Self-reflection is also essential because you will continue to evolve as you mature. There is no way around this process. It never ends. Your passions will change, and so will your values. Once upon a time, you may have dreamed of this, and now you dream of that because, over time, your desires have subtly shifted. If you aren't consciously tracking these changes within yourself, you'll wake up one day and feel utterly lost and confused about how you got where you are. "Lost and confused" is not a good state to be in for your relationship. So, as you practice constant self-reflection through journaling and contemplation, you'll discover your new needs and if these are being met. If they aren't, you can share what you've learned with your partner, and both of you can sort that out. The same applies to the other person in the relationship, of course.

Letting Helping Hands Help

While the relationship is between you and one other person, the fact remains that there will be times when you will need support. You may feel confused about some issues, and it helps to have an outside perspective to help you gain clarity. For instance, if you ever find yourself in a position where you're not feeling appreciative of your partner or your connection with them, someone on the outside could help you look at things differently and help you find the love in your heart for your significant other once more. They do this while validating your feelings, of course, but in the same breath, they will gently nudge you to see the good that you have. Friends and family can remind you that there is no such thing as a perfect relationship, and the grass will always be greener where you water it. They also have their experiences to draw on to offer you helpful insights on how to handle obstacles or challenges.

Your friends and family should always be involved in your relationship to an appropriate extent because they are people who typically share the same values as you do. You wouldn't be connected to them if you didn't have the same set of morals. So, you can think of these people as enforcers and reinforcers who ensure that your relationship continues to toe the line of those values and morals that you hold dear. It's also nice to know that in times of trouble, you can draw security and strength from the people who have known and loved you most of your life. They'll be there to cheer you on through the worst of times until you and your partner can make it out into the sunlight again. Also, if there's ever a curveball thrown at you, one that is too tough and heavy to bear on your own, these people, your friends and family will become your sanctuary. They will give you unwavering support and console you without judgment.

Conclusion

This book may have concluded, but a new chapter of your relationship has just begun. How the story ends is entirely up to you and your partner. The fact that you've read to this point is a clear indicator that you are not willing to give up on your relationship despite infidelity and its horrible effects. This is a good sign you'll pull it off in due time. You don't have to wait for the worst of times to hit before you do all you can to reinforce the positive in your relationship. With that said, it's helpful to reflect regularly on all the beautiful moments you and your partner have shared. In fact, you should go so far as to create a schedule for this sort of positive reflection. Why is this essential? Because as you constantly recall all the good things about being together, you're depositing good vibes into an emotional bank account of sorts that you can draw from when things get challenging.

The last thing you need is to struggle with a particularly bad day (or a fresh challenge) just to find your emotional bank account in the red. There is no such thing as "doing too much" when you're rescuing your relationship from doom. Refusing to put in the effort will only leave you wondering in the future if you could have done more. It is much better to know that you did all you could to keep love's flame ablaze in both your hearts.

While the tips and strategies offered in this book are created in a linear fashion, you have to recognize that healing a relationship is not a linear process. There will be ups, and there will be downs. That's the way it goes, like it or not. So rather than allow yourself to live a Pollyanna life or buy into the Disney fantasy where everything works out happily ever after with no effort on either person's part, it is much better to be prepared and brace up for the hard times to come. There's no escaping the difficult times. However, as long as you both are committed to seeing things through, it's only a matter of time before the rain stops falling and the sunshine bursts through the clouds of your relationship.

Don't spend every waking moment worrying about the tough times. Instead, be on the lookout for every little sign of progress you can detect. When you see that you and your partner are making headway with specific challenges, you owe it to each other and your relationship to pause and celebrate that with all your heart. Make a big deal out of it. Why? Because it is a big deal. Each and every sign of improvement is a cheerleader yelling at you to keep going, telling you that the light of true love, openness, honesty, vulnerability, and all the other beautiful values of a healthy relationship is ready to shine on you both. Your mutual celebration will remind you during challenges that you can't quit now because you've come so far! You deserve love in its truest form — and with time, patience, commitment, and understanding, you'll look back on this dark time one day, and it will feel like such a distant memory it could very well be someone else's life.

If you enjoyed this book, I'd greatly appreciate a review on Amazon because it helps me to create more books that people want. It would mean a lot to hear from you.

To leave a review:

1. Open your camera app.
2. Point your mobile device at the QR code.
3. The review page will appear in your web browser.

Thanks for your support!

References

Bailey, M. (2017, September 19). Why Two Is Better Than One: How to Do Goal Planning as a Couple. Www.linkedin.com. https://www.linkedin.com/pulse/why-two-better-than-one-how-do-goal-planning-couple-michele-bailey

Bickham, S. (2023, September 4). 10 Types of Intimacy in a Relationship. Choosing Therapy. https://www.choosingtherapy.com/types-of-intimacy/

Bisignano, A. (2017, September 25). 7 Ways to Practice Social Media Etiquette in Your Relationship. GoodTherapy.org Therapy Blog. https://www.goodtherapy.org/blog/7-ways-to-practice-social-media-etiquette-in-your-relationship-0925174

Carpenter, D. (2020, February 14). 3 Ways to Build Real Empathy for Others in Your Life. Verywell Mind. https://www.verywellmind.com/how-to-develop-empathy-in-relationships-1717547

Cherry, K. (2022, January 18). Why You May Have Trust Issues and How to Overcome Them. Verywell Mind. https://www.verywellmind.com/why-you-may-have-trust-issues-and-how-to-overcome-them-5215390

Cherry, K. (2023, February 22). What Is Empathy? Verywell Mind. https://www.verywellmind.com/what-is-empathy-2795562

Dodgson, L. (2018, October 24). 11 Signs Your Old Relationships are Affecting Your Current One. Business Insider. https://www.businessinsider.com/signs-your-old-relationships-are-affecting-your-current-one-2018-6

Eisenberg, S. (n.d.). Gottman Communication Assessment. Counseling | Therapy. https://www.thecenterforgrowth.com/tips/gottman-communication-assessment

Gillihan, S. J. (2023, April 4). 12 Signs a Past Trauma May Be Affecting Your Relationship | Psychology Today. Www.psychologytoday.com. https://www.psychologytoday.com/us/blog/think-act-be/202304/12-signs-a-past-trauma-may-be-affecting-your-relationship

Gould, W. R. (2023, March 7). Why Vulnerability in Relationships Is So Important. Verywell Mind. https://www.verywellmind.com/why-vulnerability-in-relationships-is-so-important-5193728

Gulotta, J. (2022, September 26). How to Build Trust in a Relationship: 22 Tips. Choosing Therapy. https://www.choosingtherapy.com/build-trust-relationship/

Hecker, D. (2014, February 13). Relationship Success: Balancing Togetherness and Individuality. HuffPost. https://www.huffpost.com/entry/relationship-success-bala_b_4776478

Jenner, N. (2023, March 22). The Concept of Individuality in a Relationship and Why It Is Essential. The Online Therapist. https://theonlinetherapist.blog/the-concept-of-individuality-in-a-relationship-and-why-it-is-essential/

Leigh, M. (2018, January 10). Setting Goals with Your Spouse + Printable Worksheet. Live Well Play Together. https://www.livewellplaytogether.com/setting-goals-with-your-spouse-2/

Lewandowski, G. W. (2021, June 10). The 10 Most Common Sources of Conflict in Relationships | Psychology Today. Www.psychologytoday.com. https://www.psychologytoday.com/us/blog/the-psychology-relationships/202106/the-10-most-common-sources-conflict-in-relationships

Loggins, B. (2021, September 27). Intimacy in Relationships: What It Is and How to Cultivate It. Verywell Mind. https://www.verywellmind.com/what-is-intimacy-in-a-relationship-5199766

Lopez, D., Baker, N., & Nenn, K. (2015). Gestalt Therapy: The Empty Chair Technique – Mental Health Recovery. Mentalhelp.net. https://www.mentalhelp.net/blogs/gestalt-therapy-the-empty-chair-technique/

Luna, K. (2018, August 9). It's Complicated: Our Relationship With Texting. https://www.apa.org/ . https://www.apa.org/news/press/releases/2018/08/relationship-texting

Mosemann, C. W. (2022, February 8). 5 Signs of Healthy Communication in a Relationship. Tidewater Physicians Multispecialty Group. https://www.mytpmg.com/5-signs-of-healthy-communication-in-a-relationship/

Narum, A. (n.d.). How to Plan for the Future in a Relationship | Remainly. Www.remainly.com. https://www.remainly.com/articles/how-plan-future-relationship

Ningthoujam, N. (2023, September 17). 6 Red Flags That Your Past Is Affecting Your Present Love Life. Healthshots.

https://www.healthshots.com/mind/emotional-health/past-relationship-affecting-current-relationship/

Pace, K. (2016). Trust Is One of the Most Important Aspects of Relationships. MSU Extension. https://www.canr.msu.edu/news/trust_is_one_of_the_most_important_aspects_of_relationships

Pace, R. (2020, March 17). 15 Reasons for Lack of Trust in a Relationship. Marriage Advice – Expert Marriage Tips & Advice. https://www.marriage.com/advice/relationship/lack-of-trust-in-a-relationship/

Pace, R. (2021, November 29). 5 Types of Conflict in Relationships and How to Deal With Them. Marriage Advice – Expert Marriage Tips & Advice. https://www.marriage.com/advice/relationship/types-of-conflict/

Relationships and Communication – Better Health Channel. (2022, February 24). Www.betterhealth.vic.gov.au. https://www.betterhealth.vic.gov.au/health/healthyliving/relationships-and-communication#importance-of-communication

Rusnak, K. (2022, April 4). Quiz: What Is Your Relationship Communication Style? | Psychology Today. Www.psychologytoday.com. https://www.psychologytoday.com/us/blog/happy-healthy-relationships/202204/quiz-what-is-your-relationship-communication-style

Rusnak, K. (2022, March 9). The Importance of Vulnerability in Healthy Relationships | Psychology Today. Www.psychologytoday.com. https://www.psychologytoday.com/us/blog/happy-healthy-relationships/202203/the-importance-vulnerability-in-healthy-relationships

Scott, E. (2022, January 25). How to Improve Your Relationships With Effective Communication Skills. Verywell Mind; Verywell Mind. https://www.verywellmind.com/managing-conflict-in-relationships-communication-tips-3144967

Smith, S. (2015, May 25). Top 5 Most Common Reasons Why Couples Stop Having Sex. Marriage Advice – Expert Marriage Tips & Advice. https://www.marriage.com/advice/intimacy/5-reasons-why-theres-intimacy-missing-in-your-marriage/

Smith, S. (2022, January 31). 15 Relationship Conflict Patterns & Common Causes. Marriage Advice – Expert Marriage Tips & Advice. https://www.marriage.com/advice/relationship/conflict-in-relationships/

Smyth, T. (2019, April 16). Common Conflicts and Red Flags for Couples – Living With Finesse. Living with Finesse. https://livingwithfinesse.com/relationship-red-flags/

Start Here: 7 Evidence-Based Approaches to Improve Your Relationship. (2021, August 26). Psych Central. https://psychcentral.com/lib/simple-steps-to-improve-your-relationship#summary

Stevens, P. (2015, February 24). 10 Barriers To Intimacy and How You Can Break Them. The Warming Tree. https://thewarmingtree.wordpress.com/2015/02/24/10-barriers-to-intimacy-and-how-you-can-break-them/

Vakos, A. (2022, February 28). How To Deal With Unresolved Issues In A Relationship: 16 Effective Tips. A Conscious Rethink. https://www.aconsciousrethink.com/18439/unresolved-issues-in-a-relationship/

What Are The Effects Of A Lack Of Intimacy In A Relationship? | TAC. (2022, August 12). The Awareness Center. https://theawarenesscentre.com/what-are-the-effects-of-a-lack-of-intimacy-in-a-relationship/

Whitney-Coulter, A. (2021, February 5). Brené Brown on What it Really Means to Trust. Mindful. https://www.mindful.org/brene-brown-on-what-it-really-means-to-trust/

Williams, R. (n.d.). 6 Steps for Repairing Trust Issues from a Couples Therapist. IE Couples Counseling. https://www.iecouplescounseling.com/blog/how-to-deal-with-trust-issues-and-insecurities

Afifi, W.A., Falato, W.L., & Weiner, J.L. (2001). Identity Concerns Following a Severe Relational Transgression: The Role of Discovery Method for the Relational Outcomes of Infidelity. Journal of Social and Personal Relationships

Apostolou, M., & Panayiotou, R. (2019). The Reasons That Prevent People from Cheating on Their Partners: An Evolutionary Account of the Propensity Not to Cheat. Personality and Individual Differences

Baskin, T.W., & Enright, R.D. (2004). Intervention Studies on Forgiveness: A Meta-Analysis. Journal of Counseling & Development

Beltrán-Morillas, A.M., Valor-Segura, I., & Expósito, F. (2019). Unforgiveness Motivations in Romantic Relationships Experiencing Infidelity: Negative Affect and Anxious Attachment to the Partner as Predictors. Frontiers in Psychology

Burnette, J.L., & Franiuk, R. (2010). Individual Differences in Implicit Theories of Relationships and Partner Fit: Predicting Forgiveness in Developing Relationships. Personality and Individual Differences

Edwards, T., Pask, E.B., Whitbred, R., & Neuendorf, K.A. (2018). The Influence of Personal, Relational, and Contextual Factors on Forgiveness Communication Following Transgressions. Personal Relationships

Finkel, E.J., Burnette, J.L., & Scissors, L.E. (2007). Vengefully Ever After: Destiny Beliefs, State Attachment Anxiety, and Forgiveness. Journal of Personality and Social Psychology

Glass, S., & Staeheli, J. C. (2007). NOT "'Just Friends'": Rebuilding Trust and Recovering Your Sanity After Infidelity. Free Press.

Harley, W. F., & Jennifer Harley Chalmers. (1998). Surviving an Affair. Fleming H. Revell.

John Mordechai Gottman, & Silver, N. (2013). What Makes Love Last? : How to Build Trust and Avoid Betrayal. Simon & Schuster Paperbacks.

Kirshenbaum, M. (2008). When Good People Have Affairs. Macmillan.

Snyder, D. K., Baucom, D. H., & Kristina Coop Gordon. (2007). Getting Past the Affair: A Program to Help You Cope, Heal, and Move On -- Together or Apart. Guilford Press.

Solomon, S. D., & Teagno, L. J. (2006). Intimacy after Infidelity: How to Rebuild and Affair-Proof Your Marriage. New Harbinger Publications.

Thompson, A. E., Capesius, D., Kulibert, D., & Doyle, R. A. (2020). Understanding Infidelity Forgiveness: An Application of Implicit Theories of Relationships. Journal of Relationships Research, 11, Article e2

Weiner-Davis, M. (2017). Healing from infidelity: the Divorce Busting Guide to Rebuilding Your Marriage After an Affair. Michele Weiner-Davis Training Corporation.

Printed in Great Britain
by Amazon

48274399R00116